Afterglow:
Signs of Continued Love

A gentle grief support book
comprised of true stories of
comforting coincidences from
those who grieve.

D0289477

Published by Quality of Life Publishing Co.

A portion of the proceeds of the sale of this book will be donated to The Penny Bear Company, a non-profit organization based in Marblehead, Massachusetts, which brings comfort and hope through hospices and children's grief camps.

Published By:

Quality of Life Publishing Co.

Naples, Florida

Quality of Life Publishing Co. specializes in clinical and grief support
publications for hospices and other end-of-life care organizations. Publishers of
Quality of Life Matters,™ an end-of-life care publication for physicians and other
clinicians, and *Timmy's Christmas Surprise,* an uplifting children's grief story
that includes bereavement tips for the holidays.

1-877-513-0099 *(toll free in U.S. only)*
1-239-513-9907 *(outside U.S.)*
1-239-513-0088 *(fax)*

www.QoLpublishing.com

ISBN 0-9675532-1-0

Cover Photo courtesy of Wendy Lindsay © 2002

afterglow...

...the glow remaining
after the light has gone,
as after sunset.

— *Webster's*
New World
College Dictionary

Dad

God took the strength of a mountain,
The majesty of a tree,
The warmth of a summer,
The calm of a quiet sea,
The generous soul of nature,
The comforting arms of night,
The wisdom of the ages,
The power of the eagle's flight,
The joy of a morning in spring,
The faith of a mustard seed,
The patience of eternity,
The depth of a family's need.
Then God combined these qualities,
And when there was nothing more to add,
God saw the masterpiece was complete.
And so God called it
"Dad."

—Author Unknown

DEDICATED

TO TWO DEAR DADS

DADDY...

Your unconditional love
and compassion
were a constant beacon
and safe harbor
for 44 years.
Your sunbeams of love and laughter
continue to light my path.

Died
April 10, 1998

BOB...

You were more than a father-in-law.
You were a friend.
Your warmth and humor
abide,
reminding me not to take myself
too seriously
during this very brief walk on earth.

Died
May 9, 1998

CONTENTS

True Stories of Comforting Coincidences from Those Who Grieve

♥ ♥ ♥

THANK YOU

It takes many hands — and many hearts — to publish a book, and I am grateful to so many who made this gentle grief support book possible.

First, my heartfelt gratitude to those who shared their stories with me. I hope I have earned your trust.

Next, a huge "thank you" to the publishing team, including Dashia Larimer, Addison Smelko, Jan Doetsch, Carole J. Greene, Mark May, Jorge Agobian, Wendy and Rob Lindsay, Dick Scott, Gayle Aull, Joyceanna J. Rautio, Jill McMahan, Ali Morrison, Rhona Saunders, Jeanne Findlater, Lorna Bell, and Carol Jankowski.

Finally, my gratitude to family and friends — especially my ever-patient husband Gerry — who provided unending support and encouragement along the way.

— Karla Wheeler

WELCOME

The book you hold in your hands is filled with comfort and hope. Each word has come directly "from the heart," shared by someone who understands what it is like to lose someone dear through death.

We come from many walks of life, cultures, and spiritual or religious beliefs. But we are united by our desire to share our stories of comforting coincidences in the hope of easing the way for you as you journey along that sacred path known as grief.

The harvest of grief is love,
and we can reap it in abundance
if we choose to stay open to it.

— Jan Carlton Doetsch, my sister,
who wrote this after our beloved father died

MY STORY
OF COMFORTING
COINCIDENCES

I thought I was an expert in grief.

After all, my chosen volunteer work for many years has been supporting patients and families facing that most difficult of situations — terminal illness.

As a hospice volunteer, I am trained not only to provide a much-needed respite for weary caregivers by visiting with dying patients, but also to serve as a grief counselor to those who are bereaved following the death of someone dear.

I have found my niche. Being invited into the inner sanctum of a family's life during such a sad and sacred time is truly a blessing for me. Each person — each encounter — enriches my life enormously, reminding me to slow down and savor every precious day.

My hospice volunteer work also provides an opportunity

to give something in return to the local hospice that enabled my grandmother — and soulmate — to die with dignity and without pain in 1987. I was with Gramma when she took her last breath and, thanks to hospice, her "transition" (as she liked to call it) was remarkably peaceful.

Ever since Gramma's beautiful death, I have been inspired by a clear mission in life: To better understand what dying patients and their families are experiencing, and to try to ease the way for them.

I am known in some circles as "the death and dying lady," the person friends and neighbors turn to for advice and support in dealing with the terminal illness or sudden death of someone dear.

WHEN IT COMES TO GRIEF, NO ONE IS AN EXPERT

I thought of myself as an expert in such matters until the spring of 1998. That's when my husband and I were bereft of not one, but two special loved ones within a four-week period.

We watched my father — a former U.S. Marine, and the epitome of physical, moral, and emotional strength — wither to skin and bones as he waged his battle with cancer. We were both very close to Daddy; he was a best friend to each of us. The prospect of facing life without this man's wise and cheerful guidance was devastating.

Then, just a week after Daddy's funeral, a phone call came from Canada — where my husband's family lives — which thrust us right back into the emotional crisis of knowing that someone we dearly loved was about to die.

We were told that my father-in-law had been hospitalized with complications from lupus, his health nemesis for many years, and that the prognosis was not good.

We were numb. How could this be happening? We had hardly begun to deal with the reality of Daddy's death, and now our other dear Dad was dying, too?

I found myself grasping for some kind of meaning from all of this. Yes, I had a deep religious faith, believing that after the body dies, the soul lives on eternally. But even my firm belief in an afterlife was not enough to comfort me. Daily life without Daddy would be hard enough, but now my other dear friend and father, Bob, was about to leave us to join Daddy in that afterlife.

My husband and I were overwhelmed by sadness. The emotional pain seemed more than I could bear, and I found myself yearning for comfort and reassurance from Daddy. For 44 years, he had been my buddy, my beacon and safe harbor.

YEARNING FOR A SIGN

That night as I lay beside our five-year-old daughter, Jenny, after tucking her into bed, I felt inconsolable — not only for myself — but for this little child. She had been the apple of my father's eye. I felt an enormous emptiness, knowing that her Grampa Dutch would never again scoop his little "Jenny Lee" up into his strong, loving arms. How on earth would we now tell Jenny that her *other* grandfather was dying?

I dug my fingernails into the palms of my hands to try to stem my flow of tears, then pleaded with Daddy to show me some kind of sign that he was okay and that his love for us all — but especially for his sweet little granddaughter — was still alive.

The floodgates of grief opened wide, and I began to sob, trying to do so quietly so as not to awaken Jenny. In between my sniffles and sobs, I thought I heard something. Was that music? It was so faint, yet it sounded sort of familiar. But where was it coming from?

I listened intently, then recognized the cheery tune of "It's A Small World After All." The lyrics were comforting: "It's a world of laughter, a world of tears; it's a world of hope, and a world of fears. There's so much that we share that it's time we're aware, it's a small world after all."

My tears turned to grins, then to prayers of gratitude, as I realized that at the exact moment I asked Daddy for a sign of his continued love, Jenny's musical toy from Disney World had mysteriously started playing from within her closet.

The unexpected tinkly music from behind a closed door struck my funny bone. It made me think of the beautiful passage read by our parish priest at Daddy's memorial service.

> Death is nothing at all. I have only slipped away into the next room. I am I, and you are you. Whatever we were to each other, that we still are. Call me by my old familiar name, speak to me in the easy way which you always used. Put no difference in your tone, wear no forced air of solemnity or sorrow. Laugh as we always laughed at the little jokes we enjoyed together. Smile, think of me, let my name be ever the household word that it always was, let it be spoken without affect, without the trace of a shadow on it. Life means all that it ever meant. It is the same as it ever was; there is unbroken continuity. Why should I be out of mind because I am out of sight? All is well. — *Henry Scott Holland (1847-1918)*

I wondered if the priest — or even the author himself — had ever imagined that the phrase, "the next room," would be taken so literally as to mean the tiny dark closet in a young child's bedroom.

Was the sudden music I heard just coincidence? Perhaps, but this synchronicity was so comforting to me that I found myself renewed. Now, I would somehow find a way to get through the coming days, as painful as they were. As my father-in-law, Bob, lay on his deathbed 1,500 miles away, my own father had given me a laugh from "the next room."

'COME ON IN. THE WATER'S FINE.'

During the next two weeks, as Bob's physical condition rapidly deteriorated, I had vivid images of Daddy reaching out his hand to his buddy, Bob. I could hear Daddy's warm, confident voice saying, "Come on in, Bob. The water's fine."

The two Dads were as much alike as they were different. They were generous, kind-hearted, charismatic men in their early 70s. Both had been married 50+ years and were devoted family men. They were known for their sunny dispositions, sincere warmth, and compassion. Both found joy and meaning in life by doing thoughtful things for others, yet I can't recall either man ever expecting praise or seeking recognition for his good deeds.

Yet they looked as dissimilar as the old cartoon characters Mutt and Jeff. Daddy was a large, deliberate man with a shiny bald head; Bob was petite and quick-witted, with a full mane of silver waves. Whenever they were together, it was like old-home week. They enjoyed each other immensely and obviously shared a special bond.

That bond strengthened with the birth of their granddaughter, Jenny, whom they both adored.

These images of Daddy gently welcoming Bob into the afterlife helped soothe my shattered heart as we lived our days on pins and needles, wondering each time the phone rang if this would be "the" call, the one informing us that Bob had died.

When Bob's death appeared imminent, my husband decided to fly to Canada to be with his family. I wanted to travel with him, as Bob and I were extremely close, but I knew my emotional health was far too fragile. So Jenny and I stayed home in Florida.

HEART-SHAPED VISION

The afternoon Bob died, I went out to our patio to tell Jenny the sad news. She was playing in the swimming pool, and I crouched down to give her a hug and tell her that

Grandpa Wheeler had just died.

I didn't know how she would respond. Having both grandfathers die back-to-back must be hard for a young child. I knew from my hospice volunteer work that we each grieve differently and in our own time. This is particularly true for children.

Jenny paused for several moments, staring at the side of the pool. Then her big brown eyes widened as she exclaimed, "Look, Mommy, there's a heart-shaped stone." I got down on all fours to look. Sure enough, embedded in the white concrete was a tiny, red, heart-shaped stone chip. It was no larger than a flea.

Then she added matter-of-factly, "And Mommy, I think it's from Grampa Dutch. No, I think it's from Grandpa Wheeler. Well, I guess it's from BOTH my grandpas. Now I know they're together and they still love me."

And with that, she turned and resumed her play.

I thought of how comforted I had been the previous week when Jenny so sweetly helped me to smile again. We were enroute to kindergarten, when a song came on the radio that reminded me of my father. I yearned for one of his bear hugs. Jenny saw my tears and asked why I was crying. "Because I miss my Daddy," I answered softly.

We drove in silence for a few miles, then Jenny said excitedly, "Look, Mommy, there's a heart-shaped cloud! And there's another one! I think Grampa Dutch is telling you that he still loves you."

The child was comforting the parent.

A Sign from Bob: Snow in Florida?

The morning after Bob died, I sat in the back yard, entering into my journal some of the many reasons I was thankful for having had Bob in my life. As I began to write about his unique sense of humor, an unexpected breeze swirled through the yard. That's odd, I thought. It was a perfectly still May morning.

I looked up, and to my delight, was suddenly showered with yellow leaves from a towering carrot tree. I smiled and said aloud, "Okay, Bob, are you trying to tell me it's snowing in Florida?" Bob loved to talk about the weather, particularly after my husband and I moved to Florida to be near my parents. Bob would call us from Canada and ask, "Any snow there today?" "None yet," we'd reply, "but we're expecting a cold front, and the temperature might dip below 80." Then we'd all laugh.

HAPPY HOUR IN HEAVEN?

One night soon after the Dads died, I had a vivid dream in which my mother-in-law and I were cooking supper for Daddy and Bob. At her request, I went into the other room to ask the men what they'd like for dinner: pot roast or fondue. I fully expected them to choose pot roast, as they were both meat-and-potatoes kinds of guys. In my dream as I entered the room, Bob saluted me with his trademark cocktail in hand. Daddy stood behind him, and I could see his glass of white Zinfandel wine on the table. I asked them which they'd prefer, pot roast or fondue, and in unison they smiled and shouted, "fondue!"

I told my mother-in-law about the dream, and we had fun joking about the fact that there must be a choice of menu in the afterlife. *And,* we agreed with glee, imagine all the folks who will be tickled pink to know that there's a Happy Hour in heaven.

CONTINUED SIGNS

It's been a few years now since Daddy and Bob died, and as difficult as it is to face each day without our Dads by our sides, the comforting coincidences seem to continue. With each occurrence, our path of grief is less painful, and we feel a renewed connection of love — love for each other and love for and from those two dear men.

And Jenny — well, her heart-shaped vision is still going strong. From her early days of seeing heart-shaped clouds and

stones, she has expanded her vision to include everything imaginable — puddles, potato chips, pieces of playground mulch, oil stains in parking lots, and dust balls. She even spotted a heart-shaped curl in my hair this past Mother's Day.

Six-year-old Jenny proudly displays two heart-shaped pickles. Each time she spots a heart-shaped item, Jenny tells me it must be another sign from her beloved grandfathers that they are together, and that they still love her.

Then there are my favorites — and hers — heart-shaped pickle slices. I'll never forget the day Jenny came skipping into my home office. "Look at this cute little heart-shaped pickle I found, Mommy. Would you like one?" Drip, drip, drip went the pickle juice onto the carpet. I looked up in annoyance. Jenny quickly added, "I'm sorry I bothered you, Mommy. I know you're working today."

I thought of the wisdom a dear friend shared at her daughter's funeral. "Never hesitate to hug your kids, because as we learned so tragically, you never know when they might leave your side."

I scooped Jenny up onto my lap. My tears of joy dripped onto her ponytail, and her pickle juice dotted my T-shirt. It was a great hug. I whispered, "I love you, my sweet, precious little daughter," to which Jenny replied, "And I love *you,* my sweet precious little mommy."

A LEGACY OF LOVE AND LAUGHTER

Immediately after the pickle incident, I got down on my knees and said a silent prayer of gratitude for this precious child who blesses our lives in endless ways. It struck me that she is the only person on earth who contains the genetic material of *both* those dear men, whose presence is so sorely missed by so many.

I knew that the magical heart connection Jenny shares with her grandfathers would be an ongoing catalyst of comfort for others. I made a vow to Daddy and Bob that I would nurture Jenny's heart-shaped vision and write about it as a way to share with others their incredible legacy of love and laughter.

MOMENTS OF SADNESS, MOMENTS OF JOY

As someone once said: "Grief is a process, not an event."

Our families have found this to be true, and we try to honor this in ourselves and each other. At Thanksgiving or Christmas dinner, for example, those empty chairs at the table can still sometimes prompt a tear. But eventually our tears turn to fond reminiscences and even laughter, as we realize the value of a story shared and bask in the warmth of love that continues to shine so brightly in our lives.

May the following stories bring you comfort. ❦

The

Stories

The stories told to me of comforting coincidences following the death of someone dear are all so very special. This one from Penny Wigglesworth of Marblehead, Massachusetts, is incredible in many ways, as you will read. It seems her husband of 41 years, who did not believe in an afterlife, is making the rounds to each family member, reassuring them of his never-ending love.

GIFF: STILL THERE FOR US ALL

The sudden death of my husband and best friend, Giff, seemed more than I could bear. After 41 years of marriage, raising four wonderful children, and welcoming seven grandsons into our lives, Giff and I led a charmed life.

But life as we happily knew it ended tragically early one morning in November while we vacationed in Southwest Florida. During the night, Giff had awakened with indigestion problems, but he took something for his stomach and settled back to sleep. He woke me up at 7 a.m., and I asked him how he was feeling. He told me he was feeling much better, so I got up to take a shower. Within minutes, I heard some horrible sounds coming from our bedroom. I ran to Giff's side and saw he was in trouble.

With the help of a very calm 911 operator, I did everything I could to keep him alive, including mouth-to-mouth resuscitation and CPR. But within minutes, as I held Giff in my arms, I knew he was gone.

The day of his death unfolded like a nightmare as I forced myself to pick up the phone and call our children, each of whom adored their Dad. This was the saddest day of our lives.

The next 10 days or so were an emotional blur for us all, with one incredible exception. It seemed that Giff was keeping quite busy since he crossed over to the other side. As unbelievable as it might sound, our Giff was making the rounds, letting each of us know that he was okay and that his love for us did not die with his body.

A NON-BELIEVER MAKES CAMEO APPEARANCES

The irony of his making contact with all of us is that while he was on earth, Giff did not believe in an afterlife. He thought that you lit the candle at birth, blew it out one day and that was the end.

Through our years together, Giff would roll his big blue

---

eyes whenever I spoke about anything of a spiritual nature, which was quite often. In fact, such topics had become my passion after I nearly died from an allergic reaction to a bee sting and had what's known as a "near-death experience."

Giff *really* rolled his eyes when I'd tell people about the glorious white light I saw, that my deceased mother came to greet me, how I knew it wasn't my time yet, and that I "came back" determined to let others know that we needn't fear death and that we will connect with our loved ones once again. My near-death experience taught me how quickly life can be over, that it's so important to enjoy every moment of every day and to live life to its fullest.

So within just days of his *own* death, my champion "roller of the eyes," that big-hearted guy who lived 70 years without ever talking about an afterlife, had done a complete 180-degree turn and was making a point of "visiting" each of us. How ironic! And how typical of Giff to make his presence known to *all* of us — with no exclusions!

MY HANDSOME YOUNG GROOM

Giff made his presence known to me in several "comforting coincidences," but the one I treasure most came in the form of a vivid dream.

In the dream, there he stood, looking as young, handsome, and trim as the day I married him. There were lots of people around, and I went up to Giff and asked, "What are you *doing* here? I thought you died." He looked at me tenderly and said, "We *never* die... love never dies."

This dream was just fabulous for me, because the picture of Giff I now have in my mind is the one from the dream. Faded is the horrible picture of him dying so traumatically in my arms.

In spirit form, Giff has made the rounds to each of our kids, and his "appearances" have brought comfort, hope, and many a laugh. His messages to our two daughters were warm and reassuring, just what Sally and Nancy needed at the time.

A HUG FROM DAD

Sally, our youngest daughter, was having a really hard time dealing with the news of her Dad's death. The night Giff died, she finally fell asleep and dreamt that a robber was coming into the bedroom. She was very scared and tried to call out to her husband, but no sounds would come. Then the person she thought was a robber lifted her up and held her in his arms. Sally felt so comforted and was no longer frightened. She felt a peace come over her.

She called me the next day and said, "Mom, I had the most amazing dream. I got the most wonderful hug from Dad last night!"

DAD'S REASSURING SMILE

Our older daughter, Nancy, told me about her dream in which she was packing up boxes and bringing them to her car. All of a sudden, her Dad drove up in his old 1988 blue Buick. He had a big smile on his face. Then he put the Buick in reverse, backed up, and drove off. In the dream, several people were standing around, looking incredulous, as they knew Giff had died. They asked Nancy, "Was that your *father*?"

Nancy and I agreed the dream was Giff's way of reassuring her that everything was going to work out just fine. Giff had been wanting Nancy and her husband to finish the house they had been working on for 10 years so they could finally move into their dream home.

Giff's "visits" to our sons still give me goosebumps, and the boys' reactions to their profound experiences warm my heart enormously. You see, like their father, the boys have never been ones to talk about an afterlife. But Giff's contacts with them were so poignant that the boys felt compelled to publicly share their experiences with the 600+ folks who packed the church Thanksgiving weekend for Giff's memorial service.

SPECIFIC INSTRUCTIONS FROM DAD

Our youngest son, Johnny, is a Navy pilot who is flying missions in Afghanistan as I write these words. While home for Giff's memorial service, he came to me one morning looking worried and asked if I knew where Giff might have put the antique gun he had. I said I knew nothing about it, and Johnny explained that he and Giff were the only ones who knew where it was kept. Johnny was distraught: the safekeeping spot was empty, and his search of the house was futile. Although the gun had no bullets, Johnny didn't want anyone to come upon it unexpectedly, as they might not know it was bulletless and harmless.

The next morning, Johnny looked rather pale. Then he told me his Dad appeared to him in a dream and gave him explicit instructions to find the gun. Giff told him, "Go downstairs, into my darkroom. Up behind the cupboard, behind some photographic equipment, wedged in between the wall and the cupboard, is a box." Johnny was still somewhat in shock. He had followed Giff's instructions, and to his amazement, discovered the gun.

MY DAD — 'MR. CAPITAL LETTERS'

Giff's method of communicating with our oldest son, Giffy, was also during dreamtime.

Amidst laughter and tears, Giffy told me the morning after his Dad's death: "You know, Mom, Dad taught me just about everything — all about business, how to ski, how to play golf. But there was one thing I taught *him* — computers. It took a lot of patience teaching Dad about computers, and it used to drive me crazy how he insisted on using all capitals when he typed an email message."

Giffy then explained how he had been dreaming during the night when suddenly his dream was interrupted by the sight of a bright white computer screen. Giffy said he was "in between dreaming and waking up" when big, bold capital letters slowly began to come across the screen, saying, "I'M O.K. TELL EVERYBODY I SAID HI."

Giffy immediately woke up, recognized the importance of what had just happened, and made a deliberate effort to re-member the exact words he had seen.

Then he lay there chuckling — because of the capital letters. As Giffy told me, "I know Dad did that on purpose. That was his style, which makes sense, because after all, Dad lived his life in capital letters!"

HIS LOVE IS STILL THERE FOR US ALL

Yes, "Mr. Capital Letters," that sweet "roller of the eyes," seems to be having a grand old time communicating with each and every one of us.

Beyond a shadow of a doubt, my kids and I know that Giff's love continues to shine. Giff and his undying love are still there for us — to comfort us, reassure us, embrace us, and bring us a smile or two.

Thank you, Giff. We will always love you, too! ❦

A bolt out of the blue... An idea that pops into our consciousness at an unexpected time ... Just coincidence? Perhaps not, says Darla Del Sasso of Bonita Springs, Florida. Here's her remarkable experience following the unexpected death of her stepfather.

THE WALLET

When I was 26, my stepfather died unexpectedly. I was filled with sadness and overwhelmed with feelings of regret.

I regretted so many things, like the fact that I had been a difficult teenager to raise. But what broke my heart most was my sense that I hadn't expressed my love and affection for Glenn while he was still alive.

As my mother coordinated plans for Glenn's cremation, I sat on the porch of their house, beating myself up for having taken Glenn for granted for so many years.

Just as I wondered aloud if he knew how much I loved him and how thankful I was to have had him as my stepfather, an image bolted into my mind. That's odd, I thought. Why do

I feel so compelled to go find Glenn's wallet? Perplexed, but somehow driven by an energy beyond my control, I went into the house to locate his wallet.

There it lay, in plain view, on the dining room table. I picked it up and began to flip through. The usual stuff was there: driver's license... credit cards. Then my heart skipped a beat. Tucked safely inside the well-worn wallet was a picture of me as a high school senior. I tenderly removed the photo and turned it over to see what — if anything — I might have inscribed on the back. My feelings of regret were transformed into utter joy and peace. Here are the words I had penned:

"To my stepfather Glenn. I hope you know how much I love you and appreciate all you have done for me." I had signed it, "Love, Darla."

The fact that Glenn had chosen to carry that photo with him for the past eight years touched my heart, and I believed without a doubt that Glenn knew I loved him. *And* I had a sense that it was his continued love for *me* that inspired me with that bolt out of the blue to find his wallet. ❧

My grandfather was a master at making me laugh through his intentional misuse or mispronunciation of words. For example, instead of saying, "I got my words mixed," he would say, "I got my mords wixed." Sherri Servin's dad must have been like that. This resident of Kailua-Kona, Hawaii, tells how her father — her "best bud" — brightens her day when things get tough.

THE FLUTTERBY

When I was a young girl, my father and I would spend hours talking about nature, space, and all things possible. He was my best bud. One day we were outside talking about UFOs, heaven, space, and what happens when we die.

About that time a butterfly went by us, and Dad said, "Look, sweetie, a flutterby!" And me being the argumentative kid I was, I said, "No, Daddy (giggle), that's a butterfly!" He said, "No, it's a flutterby – see, it flutters by," and we both laughed. From that day on we called them flutterbys.

About 18 years later, my dear Daddy died of a sudden

heart attack while I was out of town with my new family. My mother decided to have a closed casket, so I never got to see him one last time. I honored her wishes, and didn't see him. I had a very hard time with his death; I went into a deep depression.

A short time after my father died, I was out in Dad's backyard, crying and thinking about him when a flutterby fluttered by.

The flutterby went all around me, then stopped, very close. I watched it for a long time. A great feeling of peace spread over me, and a smile came to my face. It was like a message from Daddy that everything would be okay. After that I felt much better. And to this day, when things get tough for me, I see a flutterby. ♥

We talk about spending an hour to go shopping or spending time with people we love. A dear mother may reach the final moments of life and reflect on how she spent it. "A life well spent," often describes a mother's perpetual nurturing of husband, children and grandchildren. How fitting it is, then, that a welcome reassurance would come in the form of a coin for Carol Hardie of Port St. Lucie, Florida.

A NICKEL
IN THE SAND

My mother and I had a very special relationship. We often talked for hours. On a summer afternoon many years ago, my mom and I were walking along the shore in Vero Beach, Florida, sharing our thoughts and feelings. She mentioned that her health was poor. She said that when her time in this life was over, she would be able to leave gracefully. "A life well spent," she would often say, meaning that her greatest joy was her four children.

I was stunned, and somewhat frightened by her calm acceptance of her fate. My immediate response was to ask, "But Mom... who will watch over me? Who will take care of me?" My mom gave me her reassuring smile and said not to fear; she would always leave me nickels to let me know that I was still within her guidance.

The following year, my mom passed away. My grief was immeasurable. I spoke of her often — of our beautiful memories and, of course, her promise of nickels.

One Mother's Day years later, I was again walking along the shore in Vero Beach, this time with my two sons, Russ and Gary. We came upon the lifeguard stand that was once Mom's favorite spot. She had loved the security it provided. It was now tattered and worn with age.

Suddenly, we noticed a beautiful, sparkling object embedded in the sand. The reflection of the sun made it glisten and shine. To my astonishment, lying so safe and guarded in the sand was a beautiful nickel. At that moment, we knew my mom was with us. Her spirit surrounded us.

I still find shiny nickels... and they seem to appear just when I need them most. ♥

Ever gaze at an eagle or a hawk circling high above you? Watching a majestic bird glide on the wind, wings outstretched and still, can fill us with awe. Carolyn Schwenk of Annapolis, Maryland, as a hospice professional, was no stranger to death or to grief. But when her husband died, she and her sons found much-needed solace in a series of synchronicities.

SOARING WITH EAGLES

After my husband Bill died, I found my heart filled both with sadness and gratitude. I was so very sad to lose the one I loved. Yet I was also grateful for many things: that we had almost 38 years of a wonderful marriage, including the gift of two extra years after Bill's stroke; that his death was peaceful; and that we were surrounded by the love and caring of so many.

Grief, I learned, is the other side of loving someone so much.

Yet amidst such grief, just ten days after Bill died, there occurred a comforting coincidence, which helped to ease my aching heart.

I was sitting on my sister's deck, which overlooks green meadows, the city of Boulder, Colorado, craggy foothills, and the snow-capped Rocky Mountains. The sky was a gorgeous blue, with white cumulus clouds floating like cotton balls.

It was a serene, healing setting, and I was so glad that my family was near. All of a sudden, my son Scott pointed upwards, and his brother Dirk reached for the binoculars. Dirk confirmed what we all thought we could see — two golden eagles were soaring in the sunlight, and a red-tailed hawk was with them. Then, to our disbelieving eyes, at that very instant, four Air Force jets flashed by.

This incredible sight had significant meaning for all of us. The hawk had been Bill's good-luck symbol for most of his life. Plus, he had been an Air Force navigator on B-52s when he was younger and had always loved the poem "High Flight." The sight before us was like a perfect visualization of the following poem, which was read at Bill's Memorial Service:

HIGH FLIGHT

BY JOHN GILLESPIE MAGEE, JR.

Oh, I have slipped the surly bonds of earth
And danced the skies on laughter-silvered wings;
Sunward I've climbed, and joined the tumbling mirth
Of sun-split clouds - and done a hundred things
You have not dreamed of - wheeled and soared and swung

High in the sunlit silence. Hov'ring there,
I've chased the shouting wind along, and flung
My eager craft through footless halls of air.
Up, up the long, delirious, burning blue
I've topped the windswept heights with easy grace
Where never lark, or even eagle flew.
And, while with silent, lifting mind I've trod
The high untrespassed sanctity of space,
Put out my hand, and touched the face of God.

Somehow I knew that Bill was telling me that, just like the author of the poem, he was free, happy, and all was well. He was reassuring all of us who loved him that we would be okay, too, that he wouldn't really be gone from our lives. ❧

The love parents hold for a child does not depend on how long that child lived with them. Some infants come into their family's lives for mere moments, but those moments — days or weeks — shine with the radiance of a brilliant star. Alissa and Joseph Wilke of Springboro, Ohio, find the anguish of losing a cherished child can be eased somewhat by sweet memories, loving family and friends, and by comforting coincidences. Alissa remembers with love the brilliant, but painfully brief, shimmer of their son's life.

A Star Named Sam

While I was pregnant with Sam, I used to tell people that — after infertility treatments and a miscarriage — my husband and I had given up. I said Sam must have fallen from a star into my tummy. That is how we thought of him, as a little soul who fell from a star into our lives. Late at night, I would sing him to sleep with the words of a song from the 1960s: "Good morning, starshine. The earth says hello. You twinkle above us, we twinkle below."

He had lived with us for only a month, and he was the

sweetest, prettiest little boy, with the most amazing dark eyes. He hardly ever cried. We were lucky to have taken many photographs of him his first week of life. We were also fortunate that both sets of grandparents drove great distances to see Sam his first week of life. I'm so glad they got to know him.

Sam was our only child, born to us late in life, when I was 40 and my husband was 41. Baby Sam never showed any signs of his congenital heart deformity, except for poor feeding. Every time I mentioned it, I was told it was normal for a baby to fall asleep while feeding. So, we didn't know we were going to lose him until the night we took him to the emergency room.

After Sam died, an emergency room nurse named Cindy stayed with us and comforted us until we felt strong enough to drive home. We stayed another six hours before we felt we could make the trip. Cindy was there the whole time, even though I'm sure she had other duties.

A FIRST COINCIDENCE

Just as we were about to leave, Cindy noticed our home address, and stopped us. She had two close friends on our street, she said, who would be glad to stay with us. She was concerned because we were new to the area and had no relatives nearby. It turned out we already knew and liked these people. We felt funny about waking neighbors at 6 a.m. to say our baby had died, so Cindy called on our behalf.

The long drive home was awful, but when we pulled into the driveway, we were met by Cindy's friends. They stayed with us until family arrived, and helped us with difficult phone calls and funeral arrangements. When we felt lost or thought we were going crazy, they knew how to help, because they were nurses, too. What we hadn't known before, though, was that they worked at a home for mentally disabled children. Part of their job was to help parents with decisions after the loss of a child! We were in the best of hands.

TWO MONTHS LATER: COMFORT ONCE AGAIN

Sam died on April 19, 1996, and that summer, my husband and I enrolled in a Tai Chi class. We thought the Eastern form of exercise and martial arts would help balance our minds as well as our bodies. We needed something to help ease the anxiety and depression we both were experiencing.

The small class consisted mostly of people our age, with the addition of an elderly woman who drove 30 miles three times a week and never missed a class. She wore colorful tennis shoes: one night she'd sport purple, the next evening, orange.

As we walked to our cars after class one night, we stopped to introduce ourselves. She said she was taking the class to help her cope with the painful void after the recent death of her husband, who was her best friend. They even worked together.

Just as we said our goodbyes, she told us her husband's name was Sam. We could hardly believe it and asked what date he died. Her Sam died the same week as our Sam.

OUR SWEET LITTLE STAR

That Christmas my husband and I joined a support group, which was wonderful for us. One of the activities planned to help all of us who were grieving was a Christmas tree, which volunteers had decorated with ornaments carrying the name of each loved one who had died. A ceremony was held, during which we all prayed and sang. Then we said each loved one's name out loud. Afterwards, we were to find our ornament on the tree, which we were told was a different design each year. We were to take this decoration home with us.

That year — our first Christmas without Sammy — the ornament we took home with Sam's name on it was a star.

We found our way through the early grief with the help of friends, support groups, and journal writing. It has been three years since Sam died, and we are doing much better. We hope one day soon to be adoptive parents. But the coincidences of that first year comforted us and gave us the reassurance we needed that we were being cared for by the love of God and our little boy, Sam. ♥

It is said that when one soul departs, another arrives to take its place. I have stopped being surprised at the number of times people have shared with me stories of birthday and deathday connections. The joy of the one seems to help alleviate the sorrow of the other. Barbara Irwin of Cambridge, Ontario, tells us of that connection in her own family.

NONA'S BIRTHDAY GIFTS

It was on January 2, 1995 — the evening of the birth of our third child — that my step-grandmother, Nona, passed away. She was in her 90s. Throughout my third trimester, she would constantly ask, "When are you going to have this baby?" Nona spoke only Italian, so her questions had to be translated by my mother or stepfather.

Katie Ann was born at 3:46 p.m., all 10 lb., 13 oz. of

her! I remember talking with Nona on the phone (with my mother's help) from my hospital bed. She was so thrilled that I had "finally" had the baby.

The next morning, my husband called to tell me Nona had died during the night. I remember the grief that swept over me, then the panic, as I realized I would not be able to attend the funeral or assist my mom and stepfather. Then I recall feeling overwhelming pride and love, as the nurse brought my new baby to me.

Two weeks later, we all went to the movies to celebrate the birthday of our oldest child, Meaghan. It was a very cold and sunny January afternoon. Suddenly, there were screeches from the back seat, as Meaghan pointed out to all of us — Mom, Dad, Robbie, and baby Katie — the beautiful surprise in the sky: a rainbow! We could not believe our eyes. Whoever heard of a rainbow on a sunny day in January? Meg said it was probably her birthday present from Nona, and with tears in our eyes, we had to agree.

Less than two weeks after that, it was *my* birthday, and once again we were driving, though I can't remember where. I do vividly remember, however, looking out of my window at the heavens and seeing, once again, a beautiful rainbow. Nona had sent a rainbow for my birthday, too!

In my family, we all now believe that every rainbow we see is a gift from someone we love who — from heaven — is loving us back.

Minutes before I wrote this story to send to you, I'd been working on a children's story about an angel. Dear daughter Meaghan sat at a table near my desk, busily drawing a picture. When she was finished, she brought her drawing to me. It showed Abigail, the Angel — the main character in my children's story — and another angel. This one, full of wrinkles and pride, Meaghan had named Nona. ♥

As I write the introduction to this loving story from Wendy and Rob Lindsay of Guelph, Ontario, I am filled with overwhelming grief. My husband and I have been dearest friends with Wendy and Rob for almost 25 years. Their lovely daughter, Laura, and her fiance, Jonathan, were killed by a drunk driver in 1996. Just as Wendy and Rob were at a peaceful place in their grief process, another tragedy struck. Their 33-year-old son, Tim, died in an automobile accident in October 2001. They now have no living children, and their grief is more painful than any I've known. And yet they seem to have an amazing sense that their children continue to journey along together. The night Wendy and Rob called us about Tim's death, their first words were, "Our Tim has now joined our Laura." Here's the story they wrote (with Tim's help) a year ago.

LOVING LINKS
WITH LAURA AND JONATHAN

In the spring of 1996 our beautiful, vivacious daughter, Laura, and her devoted partner, Jonathan, were traveling across the deserts of Arizona north of Flagstaff. They had been on the road for six months in their sunny yellow VW camper van.

They were on a quest, visiting ancient sites linked to the emerging consciousness of mankind as part of a months-long vacation before they were to join a friend in Canada in a joint business venture. They had traveled throughout Mexico, visiting Palenque, Tulum and many smaller and lesser-known Mayan sites before they headed into Belize and the site of Tikal.

On April 9 they were returning from the Hopi's Second Mesa, within the Navajo Reserve in Arizona. As they rounded a sweeping turn and headed toward the sunset, their earthly lives ended. They were hit by a careening truck with a very drunk young man at the wheel. The fiery crash ended all three young lives.

LINKED IN TIME AND SPACE

In our devastating grief nine months later, we journeyed to Mexico to explore the area on the coast where Laura and Jonathan had camped a year earlier. Through an amazing chain of events — one person led us to another and another — until we arrived at the exact place where they had camped, played beach volleyball daily, and taken diving lessons. It was about three o'clock on a Sunday afternoon.

At the same time, our son, Tim, was in Arizona on business. He had driven out to the crash site on the Navajo Reserve and pulled up to find a truck and three native people there. The man was just finishing erecting a wooden cross in memory of his cousin, the truck driver. He told our son something he had never shared with anyone before. The man was planning to come to the reserve on his day off to get his cousin and take him to the city to help him dry out and find a job. But he got busy and postponed the trip until his next day off. Within the next week, the deadly accident happened.

Unknown to any of us at the time, he and our son stood at the crash site on the same day, at *exactly* the same time, as we found the campsite and stood talking with the young Mexican who had played beach volleyball and gone diving with Laura and Jonathan.

What are the chances of that happening at *precisely* the same time? That two highly significant places for our loved ones would be linked in time and visits by their family? It was like a reassuring "coincidence" for us.

ANOTHER COMFORTING CONNECTION

The next December, our family returned to the crash site in Arizona. This time it was my husband and I who were erecting a handmade red wooden cross in memory of our Laura and Jonathan. As we scraped and dug into the rock-hard ground, a truck pulled up, and three adults walked across the road to talk with us.

The threesome included the grandmother and another cousin of the drunk driver. They were enroute to town to visit the police station, hoping to find our address so they could mail us a Christmas card. They had the card with them, and they gave it to us there at the side of the road, at the crash site that had linked our lives forever. Another "coincidence"?

Later that same day, back in Flagstaff, we tried to locate the VW dealer Jonathan had mentioned by phone who had been so helpful to them in the days preceding the accident. We went from dealer to dealer, but most dealt only in new VWs. One dealer told us of two other shops that specialized in VW repairs.

At the last shop, an employee looked through all invoices dating back to Laura and Jonathan's trip, but his search came up empty. Just then, another shop worker came in, heard of our plight, and said, "You know, there's a chap who specializes in older VWs. I don't know where he lives, but I know his name and phone number," which he proceeded to recite from memory.

We thanked him and found a phone booth. Yes, the man definitely remembered our Laura and Jonathan, as they had

LOVING LINKS WITH LAURA AND JONATHAN

stayed with him and his family the day before they died. He invited us to come out to his place and get acquainted. He and his family were able to share with us how happy Laura and Jonathan had been and how much their love for one another was apparent. The family's recollections seemed so real that we almost expected Laura and Jonathan to walk in — if only they could have.

But we were thankful for another chain of "coincidences" that led us to reassurance and a certain serenity. ♥

Footnote: The soul-soothing photo that graces the cover of this book is from Wendy and Rob Lindsay. It was taken 22 years ago while their family vacationed at Lake Berford in Ontario. The silhouettes are those of their precious children, Tim and Laura, who always seemed to enjoy traveling along together during their short time on this earth. Wendy and Rob's grief is heartwrenching, and just when I wonder how they find the strength to carry on, an email arrives from them, and I'm once again filled with awe for these dear parents who continue to bring joy into so many lives, even when their own hearts are broken and shattered.

Wendy is a professional photojournalist who will be helping to compile stories for future editions of AFTERGLOW. See Page 171 to learn how to submit a story for consideration by Wendy and our other editors.

When I think of my grandmother, I smell sauerkraut simmering on the stove. As I recall childhood summer vacations in the Pocono Mountains, the aroma of pine trees fills my senses. Who hasn't been deeply moved by a scent that reminds us of warm, wonderful times gone by? For Shirley Griffith of Beach City, Ohio, the scent of lilacs soothes her soul and invokes memories of her mother's words of wisdom: "All in good time."

WHEN YOU SMELL LILACS

It seems as though the scent of lilacs always fills the air as Mother's Day approaches. As the youngest of 10 children, I was the baby of the family and very close to my mother. Certain memories of those early years are quite clear.

My mother was a very soft-spoken person. She was always busy back then with cooking, cleaning, and us kids, who were all still at home in our simple, framed house in rural Ohio. She never worked outside the home or had a driver's license. I can recall spring days when Mom would carry her wicker basket full of clothes up the steep basement stairs and out to the clothesline in the big backyard. Mom always stopped to smell the purple and white lilacs that grew tall on the bushes out there. With wash and other work done, she would go to the lilac bushes and carefully cut blossoms and arrange them into a large bouquet. Filling an old canning jar with water, she would set the bouquet on our kitchen table or on the nearby windowsill. The fragrance of lilacs filled the house almost as strongly as the aroma of Mom's vegetable soup simmering on the stove.

After the family moved from the big house into a mobile home, Dad suffered a massive stroke that left him completely paralyzed on his left side. Mom looked after him, rarely leaving home except for the occasional visit to her sister in the town nearby.

NEW HOME, NEW LILAC BUSHES

One Mother's Day, my sisters and I bought Mom several lilac bushes to plant in her tiny yard. One flourished outside my mom and dad's bedroom window. Mom would cut the stems and take a bouquet into Dad's room or set some on the kitchen table.

My dad passed away in June 1978, after being bedridden for 13 years. I had hoped that Mom's health would now stay strong, but she was soon diagnosed with Alzheimer's disease. I remember showing Mom the large lilac bush outside the kitchen window of my own house and telling her it hadn't bloomed in all the time I'd lived there. She said, "All in good time."

Mom passed away of congestive heart failure in July 1985. I had a terrible time dealing with the loss, crying for hours, and questioning why such a sweet person had to endure so much. As the next spring came, I was in my kitchen when I noticed that small purple buds had formed on the top of my lilac bush. As if an artist had taken a paint brush and spread color over a canvas, my entire lilac bush was covered with blooms.

When I went outside, the scent of lilacs seemed to fill the entire neighborhood. I carefully snipped several of the branches, brought up an old canning jar from the basement, and set the bouquet in front of me on the kitchen table. As I sat glancing at the blooms while I worked, the fragrance filled the air and I felt a peace come over me. It has been nearly 15 years now since my mom passed away, and the lilac bush has continued to bloom each spring, as if it received a touch from heaven. I'm sure that this was my mom's special way of letting me know everything would be just fine: "All in good time." ❧

Reminders of loved ones who have died come in all manner of ways. Often, people keep their stories locked inside, for fear that if they share them, others will think they're "losing it." I agree that it takes courage to share such stories. I'm glad that Janet Corking of Cambridge, Ontario, decided to share hers. She sincerely hopes these three stories will bring you a ray of hope and an ounce of comfort.

JANET'S STORY 1:

GILLIGAN'S ISLAND

There was a time when I didn't share certain experiences for fear of people thinking I was "losing it." I now realize, however, that it's helping me heal.

I lost my son, Jonathan, in September 1996, 12 days before his 18th birthday. His death was tragic and extremely painful for my whole family. I wished a thousand times that I had kept a journal, if only to recap and look at the progress we have made. Of course, the grieving process is continuing and I am sure in my case it will last my lifetime, but we are all trying to accept reality and to continue on with our lives.

Although I never kept a journal, I did jot down a few incidences (or coincidences) that made me instantly connect with my son. I do not see him or hear him or even feel his presence, but I have had some experiences which, at the time, seemed to make my grief more painful. These events now calm me and bring a smile to my face.

TWO THUMBS UP

My first experience took the form of a dream, the like of which I have never had before or since. This occurred one month after Jonathan's death.

My door slammed shut, and there stood Jonathan in his black jeans, holding his shirt in hand. I knew he had died, and I went to him and hugged him. I followed him to his room and stroked his hair and face. I could actually "feel" his presence in my dream, which was incredibly comforting. I asked him if he was okay. "Yeah, yeah," he said, as if humoring me, and then he was gone.

I was devastated by this and flung back the covers. There he was again, and I continued to touch him, asking him if he was okay. He smiled at me, never spoke, but put up both of his thumbs! The dream ended as my cat's meowing woke me.

A Christmas Excerpt

The summer before Jonathan died, we took him to the UK for vacation. We have a wonderful video of this holiday, for which I have counted my blessings many times.

In December 1996, I was watching the video. I watched for about 15 minutes, then I started to cry. When I looked up again, the VCR was playing the part in which we were in a relative's garden. Jonathan had on a silly hat and I asked him to say some words of wisdom into the camera. He lifted the hat from his head and said, "Hat."

"Okay," I said, "don't be silly," and as I moved the camera off him he said, "I am Gilligan on Gilligan's Island!" At this point exactly I switched off the VCR. The TV came on automatically and guess what was on? *Gilligan's Island!* It was a 15-second clip, an excerpt from a Christmas special.

These are things to be joyous about and know that our loved ones are always with us in some way. ♥

Janet's Story 2:

No Ordinary Seaman

For his birthday, my husband, Bill, received a gift certificate for a local bookstore. His hobby is ships. He went to get a specific book but it wasn't available. As he passed the history section, he was drawn to a book called *U-Boat Peril*. It was not really in his area of interest, but the name of the author somehow tugged on his memory. He opened the book and found that it was a story of events on the ship *The Wanderer* during the World War II years. It was written by the captain. Bill didn't have his glasses with him, so he couldn't look closely, but he decided to buy it just for nostalgia's sake.

When he got the book home, he was flabbergasted to find a picture of the ship's crew, taken in 1939. His dad was in the picture! His dad died in 1977, and while Bill knew he had been in the Navy during the war and was on that ship, he really never in a million years expected to be looking at a photo of his father – an ordinary seaman. ❧

JANET'S STORY 3:

GRANDMA'S CUTE CONNECTION

My boss, a dentist, got a new Norman Rockwell picture for his surgery room. It depicts heads of men and women who are having fun gossiping. One of these heads — I swear — looks just like my grandmother Hardy. My Mum agrees and was blown away by the likeness. So every workday, I see the picture and think of my Grandma Hardy.

One night I had a dream about Grandma's house. I had borrowed a car from my co-worker, Donna. Then I drove the car — a Volkswagen Cabriolet — into Grandma's garden. In the dream, Grandma tells me off the next morning for leaving the top down on the car and getting the seats damp.

The dream was comforting to me, as I have fond memories of time spent at Grandma's house. At work that morning, I was telling my boss about the dream, commenting on how delightful it was to be at Grandma's again, even if only in a dream.

Imagine my surprise when Donna came to work complaining about how annoyed she was with her husband. It seems he had left the top down on her Volkswagen Cabriolet the previous night, and her seats got wet. She had to sit on damp towels as she drove to work.

Such happenings, which provide a spiritual connection to our loved ones, bring me great comfort and fill my heart with gratitude. ♥

I'll bet everyone you know can tell you instantly the date of their birth. In most people's calendars, it's a special day, one when good things happen, year after year. For some people, I've discovered, the death of a certain loved one also becomes a special day — another date on the calendar when they can depend on good occurrences, year after year. Bonita Springs, Florida, resident Beverly Herron tells us of such a date on her calendar.

DAD'S FAVORITE DAY

On August 6, 1980, my darling father left this world for his eternity with Our Lord. That date represents several joyous occasions in my family.

On August 6, 1984, I passed my test for a driver's license at the ripe old age of 47! I was a physical wreck that day. My neighbor drove me to the Oklahoma highway patrol station where an armed patrolman took me out for my test. Intimidating for me? You bet! But in my hand I held a rosary made from the roses on my father's casket four years prior. Those beads were swinging and swaying from my right hand as — I passed the test! That was my dad's intercession, for sure.

On August 6, 1999, my dear husband had open-heart surgery, a five-way bypass. I prayed to my dad to intercede for us in bringing my Art through it all. I felt peaceful in my heart the entire long day and sure enough, Our Lord pulled him through safely and successfully.

August 6th is a special date in my book. My dad is still looking after his daughter from the other side. How comforting to know I have two fathers watching out for me! ♥

How could a mysterious disappearance, the revelation of a name and a recurring number all have something in common? The coincidences that bring solace to those who grieve come in all forms. These are just three that happened to Andrea McDonald of Milton, Massachusetts. "I was 26 when my mother died and 29 when my father died. Nothing brings more peace than hearing stories of comforting coincidences, except for experiencing them myself."

ANDREA'S STORY 1:

COLIN'S
HOCKEY SAVE

My husband's brother passed away in a car accident when he was in high school. Every year, the private school he attended holds an ice hockey game in his honor. "The Colin McDonald Award" is presented afterwards, usually by the family.

One year during the game, a puck was slammed full force

into the stands. It was headed straight for my niece's head. My husband, among many others, reached out to deflect the puck. But it mysteriously disappeared and was never found!

Just coincidence? We choose to believe it was Colin's lucky hockey save. ♥

ANDREA'S STORY 2:

GUSTAF'S SURPRISE

A few days after my mother's death, I found myself looking for comforting reading material on life after death and near-death experiences. I had chosen a few likely books at a local bookstore. Just as I was sitting down to read, I glanced for the first time at my mother's death certificate. I noticed that my grandfather's name was listed as Gustaf Stromberg. I thought this was odd, because I had always thought his name was Wally, or Wallace. My father said, "No, his name was Gustaf, they just called him Wally."

All of these years, and I had never even heard the name Gustaf. A few minutes later, I opened a book called *To Dance with Angels* by Don and Linda Pendleton. I turned to the index to see if there was anything in the book on near-death experiences or life after death. Imagine my surprise when my eyes landed on the name of another author in this field: Gustaf Stromberg!

Not only had I learned my grandfather's real name, but moments later I'd discovered that same unusual name in a book on life after death! This coincidence brought me enormous solace. ❧

ANDREA'S STORY 3:

GRANDMOTHER'S NUMBER

My grandmother's house number was 376. After her death, the number always seemed to surface on anniversaries, birthdays, holidays, and other special events. I believe this was her way of letting us know she is still with us.

One instance stands out. My father, whom my niece Danielle called "BJ," used to take Danielle to Toys 'R Us quite regularly, letting her pick out whatever she wanted. BJ and Danielle were very close, and these outings together were quite special for both of them.

Shortly after our father's death, my sister and I took Danielle to Toys 'R Us. When we pulled into the parking lot, we were shocked! The license plate on the car in the space in front of us was 376 BJ. ❤

Ever meet someone in an elevator or on a short walk across an intersection and find yourself somehow different after the encounter? I have. Maybe it was that person's smile, or the jaunty way he wore his cap, or the tune he whistled that lifted me up just a little. Whatever it was, I was "better" after the 30 seconds of our coming together, as if I carried a bit of their joyful spirit with me. Imagine, then, the immense influence of a loving grandparent — the kind whose spirit remains with his grandchild forever. That's what Cathy Silva of Pembroke Pines, Florida, experienced.

GRAMPA'S STAR

Some people enter our lives and connect with us so deeply that when they leave, their spirit becomes a part of us. My grandfather, Lawrence E. Johnson, was one of those people. Don't mistake me – I believe that *everyone* we encounter, however briefly, has some influence on how we think or who we become. People like Grampa, however, depart human life yet remain with us as pure love.

Grampa's life roles were varied: stone mason, record-breaking Olympic athlete, student of theology and life. His last vocation and passion was that of "gentleman Maine lobsterman." In his late 80s he was still hauling lobster traps from his little boat. Until he retired, he was the picture of health and vitality. Then he stopped living his dream, stopped going out on his boat or traveling to his favorite places of inspiration. That's when he became ill. The bone spurs in his throat made him too ill to enjoy food, another passion of his. His energy decreased to the point he could barely get out of his chair.

LESSONS LINED IN SILVER

Grampa taught me many lessons. One was that "every cloud has a silver lining." The silver lining in Grampa's deteriorating health was the time he and I could now spend together talking and philosophizing about life — its many adventures and wonders. Although at times he could barely speak and I could hardly hear him, we somehow understood one another. We were no longer grandfather and granddaughter, but two souls connecting. I found myself growing as never before.

When I felt confused or lost, I would find peace and love in connecting with Grampa. He saw me through many challenges: my separation from my husband and our reunion; my testing of my independence; and my discovery of who I am and why I'm here.

Grampa died at the age of 90, after a week-long stay in the hospital. I spent many hours with him during that journey. As he wished, he was surrounded by family and friends; all those whose lives he had touched deeply came to visit and bid him farewell. It was a long week, and he fought to stay alive, seeming to resist leaving his body. Then he slipped into a coma and his heart slowly stopped beating. He left this life surrounded by his family, all of us embracing him with the love he showed us.

Once back at Mom's house I sat by a large picture window, exhausted from the week. I felt relief and joy, knowing Grampa was free. I wondered why what I felt, though not sorrow, was so intense that it made me weep. Staring out into the dark sky, I suddenly noticed a star I had never seen before. I knew immediately that it was Grampa. The energy of his spirit was so intense that it showed as a star, and now it was free to fill every crevice of the universe.

My husband and I often sit outside now with the children, admiring "Grampa's Star." Wherever I go, I feel he is with me, sharing his wisdom and his love. He is forever my mentor, my teacher – Grampa. ❦

The natural sequence of life dictates that the child buries the parent. When it happens the other way around, sometimes grief becomes so deep that solace seems beyond one's grasp. However, hope can hover very close and wait for the right moment to show itself. Bereaved mother Eileen Shanon of Salt Lake City, Utah, found both consolation and hope from unexpected visits by hummingbirds.

WINGS OF HOPE

When our son Jason entered our garage one day years ago, he found a beautiful hummingbird frantically and determinedly beating against the clear glass window pane in a vain effort to escape to freedom. Instinctively, drawing upon his close relationship with nature, Jason put out his finger as a perch for the hummingbird. To his surprise, the hummingbird responded by resting on Jason's finger, where it remained until Jason carried it to freedom.

In the ensuing years, Jason developed melanoma. He waged a courageous battle against this often-fatal form of skin cancer, undergoing surgery, biotherapy, and chemotherapy.

It appeared that Jason was winning the battle. He and his beloved Carly got married, and they began their life together with all the dreams and hopes for the future that young people have.

But Jason's battle with melanoma was not over. This aggressive cancer returned with a vengeance, and our son lost his years-long battle.

HOPE COMES CALLING

A few weeks after his death, I sat on the patio, numb with grief. A hummingbird flew up to me and hovered in front of my face for a few seconds. Several days later, while I visited at a friend's house, a hummingbird again hovered close to my face.

Sometime later, Jason's widow, Carly, told me about her own experience. She was visiting his gravesite, the first time she had been able to do so. She knelt and wept, pleading with Jason to give her a sign that he was okay. A hummingbird flew up to her and fluttered in front of her.

I cried as Carly related this incident to me, remembering the day when Jason so lovingly freed the hummingbird that had become trapped in our garage. My crying brought my husband, Ilan, to my side. He had come in from the patio, and he told me he had prayed to the heavens for a sign to help me with the depths of my grief.

At that very moment, a hummingbird came on the scene and fluttered before us. We looked up and saw a shooting star soaring across the dark sky.

I know now that somewhere, Jason, whose wonderful smile always lit up a room, is alive, happy, and well. He is greatly missed, but I feel him all around me, and I find serenity in these comforting coincidences.

I pray that my story will help all those who have lost loved ones — and those who are afflicted with deadly diseases like melanoma — to find solace. I shall always look upon hummingbirds with love and affection and think of them as the "wings of hope." ♥

When a family is doubly bereaved, as my husband and I were when our fathers died just a month apart, we often find ourselves desperate for a sign that they are "okay" and that their love continues to shine. Following the back-to-back deaths of her father and sister, Joanne Stahlman of Naples, Florida, needed such a sign. A rainbow, interpreted by many as a promise from God, turned out to be just the thing. What could be better than a rainbow? Why, a double one, of course!

MARY ANN'S
RAINBOWS

One afternoon, while my sister Mary Ann was visiting my two young children and me, we happened to look out the French doors of the family room to see a beautiful rainbow soaring across our back yard.

Mary Ann and I took the children's hands and led them out onto the pool patio so we could see the splendor of the entire rainbow. We were delighted to see that there was not just one rainbow now, but a double rainbow!

We told my daughter and son that it was a sign from Papa, our dad and their grandfather, who had died recently following a noble fight with cancer. We said Papa was telling us that he was in heaven and that he loves us very much.

We continued to hold hands, saying a prayer together.

GOOD NEWS: SURGERY IS SCHEDULED

Three months later, Mary Ann telephoned with exciting news. She had been approved for an elective surgery, a stomach bypass, which would finally enable her to conquer the weight problem that had plagued her all her life.

The night before her surgery, we had a long phone conversation, laughing and making plans for her future, which we agreed would surely be one of lasting health and happiness.

After the operation was complete, her doctor called to let me know all had gone well. Family members had already begun visiting Mary Ann in the hospital, offering their enthusiastic support for her bright future.

The morning that my husband and I were to bring her home from the hospital, we received an emergency call from her doctor. Mary Ann had taken an abrupt turn for the worse and was to have immediate surgery.

After four grueling hours on the operating table, Mary Ann was given only a 50-50 chance of surviving. Her surgery had failed, and she had developed septic shock, an often-fatal condition.

My mother and nine brothers and sisters kept watch 'round the clock, praying that Mary Ann would somehow pull through. But for three weeks, her condition declined, and she never recovered.

SHOCK AND THE DEPTHS OF GRIEF

We were in shock: my once-healthy 44-year-old sister, who went into the hospital for an elective surgery, was now dead. All of us were doubly grieved, having just recently lost my father, and now our precious Mary Ann was gone, too.

Somehow God gave all of us the strength to get through the funeral and tend to the many matters before us.

A few weeks after my sister's death, I found myself on my knees in church, saying to Mary Ann, "Please give me a sign that you are okay and that you are in heaven. I really need to know you are at peace."

The next day was a rainy one, and my husband, daughter, son, and I were driving home when I happened to look out the car window in time to see a lovely rainbow. We all commented on its beauty.

As I walked into the house, I began to head for the pool patio. Through the French doors, I could see not just one rainbow, but a double rainbow! I screamed to my husband and children, crying, "Mary Ann sent me a sign — look! Double rainbows!"

At that moment, I remembered standing on that exact spot on the patio with Mary Ann just weeks before, as she and I told my children that the double rainbow we saw was a sign from Papa that he was okay.

I knew my dear sister was now giving me the same sign, with the same reassuring message: she was in heaven, and she was truly at peace. As tears rolled down my cheeks, I knew in my heart that even though our loved ones are gone from our sight, they are still miraculously with us. ❥

As a mother, I get all warm and fuzzy when I recall the happy anticipation I felt during my pregnancy. The promise of new life — of seeing this little person I'd already bonded with — brought rejoicing at the time and continues to thrill me in recollection. I could only imagine the stark grief that must accompany the loss of a baby through miscarriage or stillbirth. Here, Kimberly Baltzell of Kettering, Ohio, shares her painful story, which validates that every loss needs to be honored and mourned.

KYLE'S SIGN

I believe that stillbirths and miscarriages are totally overlooked in our culture. Few people seem to understand or respect how devastated a mother can feel. Many people do not consider a stillborn or miscarried baby a person and are astounded when the mother grieves.

Our third son, Kyle Edward Baltzell, was stillborn at 16 weeks gestation on July 10, 1995. The emotional pain was overwhelming. It was particularly difficult for me, because most people could not comprehend my grief. I received such comments as: "You have two other children, you're lucky because some people have none," and "Good thing 'it' died so soon. At least you didn't carry 'it' for nine months and then lose 'it.'"

HE WAS MY SON, TOO

My response is, I'm very thankful for my living children, but they do not replace Kyle. He was my son, too. If I had carried him longer, I would have been able to see the color of his hair, and there would be a grave for me to go to when I am thinking of him.

Kyle was born still more than seven hours after my labor began at 8:30 a.m. He was born at 4:13 p.m. He weighed 0.6 lb. and was 4 1/4 inches long. He had 10 tiny fingers and 10 tiny toes, complete with fingernails and toenails. His arms were holding his belly as if he had a tummy ache. We held him and had him blessed. An autopsy was performed, but no reason for his death was discovered, and his body was cremated by the hospital. We held a memorial service. We also had a tree planted in his honor at a nearby park.

We have since had another child, a daughter. Our lives have gone on and I am dedicated to my three living children. Grief does not overwhelm our lives, but I think of Kyle several times a day and frequently drive by his tree. His picture hangs in our bedroom and my mommy necklace includes a charm for him. Many people see my including him in the family as strange, but he is a real and separate person to me. He was not "just a clump of cells," or "just a lost pregnancy." He was my son!

WHO IS HEAVEN FOR?

I believe Kyle sent me a sign. After attending the funeral of a friend's daughter who was stillborn, my husband and I were extremely upset. I cried a lot, thought of Kyle, and wondered if he and my friend's daughter existed in heaven or if, as some people believe, they were too young to go to heaven.

The funeral was in an unfamiliar town, and my husband decided to take a different route back from the cemetery. When he stopped for a soda pop, I sat in the car crying.

Then I looked up and saw a sign with the word KYLE in big, red letters. It turned out to be the name of a veterinary practice. I took that as a message from my son that his soul *is* in heaven. This sign has given me great comfort.

The death of any child is indeed the toughest loss to suffer. Although my grief is not as intense as it was, I will never forget Kyle. Our souls are bonded forever! ♥

*I live in Naples, Florida, often referred to as the lightning
capital of the world. During the summer rainy season, when
we can almost count on an afternoon thunderstorm, I ignore
most thunderclaps — unless one is unusually loud or close.
Then, I really pay attention. Hospice nurse Marianne
Coddington of Richmond, Virginia, describes just such an
attention-getter in her story of a family looking for
consolation.*

NIGHT MUSIC

Subtlety was not seven-year-old Laurie's strong point.
Her losing battle with leukemia had left her very thin and very
bald, but the fine bone structure of her face and her large,
brown eyes suggested the beauty she should have grown into.
Those expressive eyes were fixed on me during my first visit
as her hospice nurse.

"We don't need you!" she said flatly. "Mommy and Daddy
can take care of me and I'm very tired of being poked by
nurses, so you can leave now." Gail and Simon, her parents,
were accustomed to her bluntness and explained to her that I

---

was there to make sure she wouldn't hurt or feel sick to her stomach anymore. She grudgingly accepted this, but after each visit I was politely informed that I could leave now.

FIXED ON A FEELING

As Laurie's disease progressed, my visits increased. Now totally bedbound in the room so lovingly decorated with characters from Sesame Street, Laurie had developed the habit of staring fixedly at the blank ceiling. When we asked her what she was looking at, she always answered, "Nothing," and went back to fixate on the ceiling.

Simon offered to put a picture of her beloved Kermit the Frog on the ceiling so she would have something to look at, but her reply was a vehement, "No!"

During her last days, consciousness came and went, but when her eyes were open they were fixed on the ceiling. Finally, she lapsed into total unconsciousness. It was as she took her very last breath that Laurie's eyes opened and she looked again to the ceiling and smiled. She uttered her last words: "Jesus comes!"

Without a doubt, those last words brought comfort to Gail and Simon, but bereavement was a rocky road for them. Gail desperately wanted a sign that Laurie was in heaven and happy. I visited them frequently. Gail reported there had been some little signs, but it somehow wasn't enough to give her the assurance she so badly needed.

One morning, about three months after Laurie's death, I received an excited call from Gail to come see them.

A BOLD STROKE

They told me that they had been having a bad night. Neither could sleep and they sorrowfully held each other, sharing tears over their lost child. "Suddenly," Gail related, "the whole house shook with a single clap of thunder and there was no thunderstorm, not even one forecast. We heard a sound from Laurie's room. It was closed up just as she left it. We got up and opened the door and on the top shelf of her bookcase her favorite music box was playing 'Lara's Theme'!"

Holding hands, Gail and Simon beamed at me. "Our little girl is fine!" At last I saw a look of peace on both their faces. For once I blessed Laurie's lack of subtlety. ♥

When I think about all the stories people have shared with me, I realize that many of them revolve around some object that was significant in their loved one's life. Jaudon Cline of Salisbury, North Carolina, defines the objects in her father's life, which brought reassurance and a sense of closure following his death.

TRAINS, BOATS AND SEAGULLS

My dad was raised in a North Carolina railroad town in the 1940s. As a young man, he served an apprenticeship on a train for four years. He loved trains and collected models of them all his life.

Dad also spent 20 years in the Air Force, where he was called Bollings' Old Man of the Sea. He was a boatmaster while stationed at Bollings, and five days a week he would operate a yacht carrying generals and colonels to and from the Pentagon. He loved his job. For 18 of his 20 years in the service, he spent nearly the entire time on, over, across, in or near the water.

On the day before his funeral, we gathered for a family dinner at Dad's retirement home in North Carolina. He had built a small lake behind his house so he could fish from the deck or just sit and admire the sunset. We sat together on Dad's deck talking about old times, when about 50 seagulls flew in and landed on the water, only to take off again as quickly as they appeared. Dad's wife said there had never been seagulls on the lake before. We all felt that this was a sign from Dad that he was okay, that his spirit was soaring with those seagulls.

We buried Dad the next day in the National Cemetery in Salisbury. You do not choose a site there, as you are given the next available spot. Well, Dad was placed 50 yards from a railroad track! During the funeral service, two trains went by just a-blowing their whistles. The ministers had to stop talking because they couldn't be heard. I knew this was again Dad's way of saying, "Hey Jaudon, don't cry for me, I'm just fine!"

It is almost the anniversary of my dad's death, but in my heart I know he is okay. The seagulls and trains provided reassurance for me. ❦

What does a person in a coma perceive? While no one knows for certain, I believe our loved ones can hear us and sense our presence. As a hospice volunteer, I often encourage family members to talk, pray, sing, play music, and even laugh at their loved ones' bedsides. Joni Hafley of Yorktown, Virginia, spent such precious moments with her mother and felt grateful when her mom later reaffirmed their unending connection of love.

MOM'S TURN
TO BE AN ANGEL

Our mom was extraordinary. At the age of 30, she married a German man she met while serving in the American Red Cross during World War II. They lived in Pennsylvania and ran their business, a small printing company, while raising six children. Mom always worked very hard. She was a talented pianist and a marvelous writer who was working on a book when she died.

In September, I got a call from my dad in the middle of the night. Mom had fainted and fallen, and was being rushed to the hospital. The family started flying and driving in from all over the country, but by the time we were assembled, she was on life support. A blood vessel had broken in her brain, and because she was on a blood thinner, there was no hope, even with surgery. We all spent the day talking to her, playing Chopin tapes, and praying.

The next day, Mom's kidneys failed. Her sister got to the hospital just in time for our father's difficult decision to turn off her life support. Incredibly, after her breathing tube was removed, her heart continued to beat for 45 minutes.

The nurse came in with a dozen roses and a fax from a grandchild in California. The fax read, "Oma, it's your turn to be an angel now."

My sister and I rode back to the house together. We were surprised to see it had rained, as the town had been suffering a drought all summer. We commented that now that Mom died, it figured we would have the gift of rain. My sister said, "Wouldn't it be great if we saw a rainbow? Then we would know she got to heaven."

That made me feel sadder, because, with this drought, I knew my sister would be disappointed. Not five minutes later, we saw the most beautiful, complete rainbow ever prismed! Now, every time we see a rainbow, we feel comforted. ♥

Buttons. We push buttons everywhere these days— on our remote control to open the garage door, the microwave oven to cook dinner, our remote to manage our TV watching, our car door to activate the locks, our camera to snap a picture. Sometimes, those we love even "push our buttons," in ways that remind us of certain habits. Both these stories provided by Sandra Hancock Martin of Montvale, New Jersey, describe what William James calls "ineffable experiences" — about buttons.

SANDRA'S STORY 1:

THE TIMEKEEPER

My mother was always on time. I was always late. She considered it unacceptable to keep someone waiting. So I grew up hearing, "Don't keep your father waiting." When I got married, she changed it to, "Don't keep your husband waiting."

Throughout my life, even after I was married, she had a way of checking on my tardiness. She would call to let me know she was completely packed a week in advance of a trip she was to take. She would call the night before *I* was taking a trip, interrupting my frantic, last-minute packing to ask, "Why didn't you do this earlier?" This question seemed to fit many situations.

Do It Now!

My mother never worked outside the house after she was married, and she did not understand how I, even with a full-time job, could feel super-efficient baking cookies on Christmas Eve afternoon for my two children to put out for Santa that night. She just could not understand why I would wait so long.

In late September of 1983, my mother was diagnosed with advanced colon cancer. We buried her on All Souls Day in early November, the day she had planned to leave for a trip to Greece with my father. She took another trip instead, and I'm not so sure she was ready this time.

My sister in California and I had been taking turns going to be with my mother in Virginia. We had asked the doctor to let us know if she started failing fast, so we could both be there the last few days. The doctor called to warn us late one afternoon, and my husband and I planned to begin the eight-hour drive first thing next morning.

NO TIME
TO SAY GOODBYE

Then at 2:00 a.m., I was called again. She was gone. My aunt said later that my mother knew we were all coming, and she didn't want to keep anyone waiting around for her to die. But we didn't get to say goodbye.

Early the next morning, we left for Virginia to be with my father. When we were an hour away from home, my husband realized he had forgotten to pack the trousers to his suit, and we had to turn around and go back for them. As we approached the house, I told my husband I would run inside with him to phone Daddy about our delay. "Oh, no," he said. "You'll find five other things to do and we'll be even later."

Just then, the lock button on my car door popped up without my touching it. Our sons in the backseat and I looked at it in amazement. I laughed out loud and said, "That's Mother, telling me one more time not to keep anyone waiting."

My husband insisted we had hit a bump, but in the 15 years we owned that car, it had never happened before, and it never happened again. My mother just could not resist telling me she was still around... and not to keep anyone waiting. ♥

SANDRA'S STORY 2:

THE PEACEMAKER

My mother-in-law was a no-nonsense woman from Michigan who had taught at an all-boys' school, served as a school principal, and reared three highly successful sons very efficiently. She did not know what to do with me — her first daughter-in-law, and the product of an emotional Southern family.

The first year of our marriage, my husband and I lived near his parents and visited them often. It was not until Christmas that my husband saw my home in Texas for the first time. Unfortunately, we did not get there precisely on Christmas Day as planned, because my husband hit a police car on a rain-soaked road, and we ended up spending two weeks in a Louisiana hospital.

WHAT FACE?
I DON'T SEE IT

One thing that I do remember about that Christmas was a card my in-laws received from their minister. It was an aerial photograph, which was said to reveal the face of Christ. My in-laws said they clearly saw the face. My husband and I did not. I still have the card and I still do not see the face.

As the years passed, my mother-in-law and I got along less and less well. I felt that she did not care for me at all and I grew to really dislike her. I used to joke that when she died, met St. Peter, and went through her "life review," she would finally realize how much she had hurt me. In her last years, she suffered from Alzheimer's disease.

In February of 1995, my husband and I left on a long-dreamed-of trip to Rome. On our first full day there, we got a call from my husband's brother, a doctor in California, telling us that their mother had pneumonia. I asked my husband if he wanted to end the trip, but he believed that she would soon recover and said no. That night, I looked at the chandelier over my head and said that if she died in the night it would surely fall on me. She did indeed die on the fifth day of our seven-day trip. The chandelier stayed up.

After hearing the news, we tried to get an earlier flight home, but could not. So, we went to the Spanish Steps. My camera, which I was always very careful with, clicked — to my surprise. I expected a photo of my shoe, but what I ended up with was a photo of the clouds over Rome. A puzzlingly familiar face took shape in the clouds.

NOW I SEE IT

In my study, I have a copy of a Ribera painting of St. Peter and St. Paul. It was the face of St. Paul that I saw in my clouds photo. I have always loved St. Paul, because of his life change. I had been angry with my mother-in-law, just as he had been angry in his youth. After the day of the St. Paul-in-the-clouds photo, I never felt anger toward her again. I felt that she pushed the button and took that photograph as a way of finally making peace between us. ❤

So often, these days, we hear stories about the heartbreak of watching a beloved relative slip from us because of severe mental deterioration. To see what once was an active — even brilliant — mind cease to function can be one of life's cruelest experiences. But like all life's tough challenges, this one can also be overcome. Sybil Nassau of Naples, Florida, tells us how she found serenity during and after her father's valiant battle with Alzheimer's disease.

MY DAD, MY FRIEND

Like many daughters, I was very close to my dad. He was the stronger parent when I was growing up, and when I was a teenager and couldn't get along with my mom, he became my stalwart friend. That bond endured for the rest of his life.

After my mom died, Dad and I were inseparable. He loved mealtimes, so he and I would often meet for lunch. On weekends, my husband and I took him everywhere with us. When Dad's progressive dementia made it necessary, we moved him to a retirement home where he would be near friends and family. Later, when he became difficult to care for, he moved again, into a very expensive locked unit.

PAINFUL TO WATCH

Dad had been a brilliant, well-known attorney, so to watch his mind deteriorating was worse than painful. Although he maintained his physical health by swimming every day until he was 90, his mental capacities began to diminish two years before his death. He became violent at times and actually threw a night nurse across the room when she tried to put on his pajamas. Yet he could whistle, sing, and dance with all of the nurses at parties. He insisted on wearing a suit and tie until just days before he died.

On Father's Day, we went to visit Dad. During lunch he kept pointing to my husband to feed him, because he wanted me to hold his hand. He refused to smile when I tried to take a picture of him with my children and grandchildren. I told the nurse that it wouldn't be long now. Dad had made up his mind that he would die soon. I went home and packed a suitcase.

The next morning the nurse called to tell me Dad had pushed away his breakfast tray. I knew what that meant, and we left right away. His eyes lit up when he saw me; he gripped my hand and hugged me.

In his remaining hours, I never left Dad's side unless he was sleeping. I tuned the radio to classical music and read his favorite poetry to him. I took over for his nurses and bathed him, medicated him, and spooned ice chips onto his tongue.

IT'S OKAY TO GO

The following evening, he suddenly stared at me and gripped my hand. I closed the windows, lowered the shades, climbed into bed with him, and wrapped him in my arms.

Unlike my mom, who had died in pain and alone, my father knew I would not leave him, and that I loved him. I sang to him and gave him permission to leave this earth to join my mom.

Just then, the curtains moved and an unexplainable strong breeze blew through the room. Moments later, Dad drew his last breath. Several of the nurses stood in the doorway crying. They also saw the breeze move the curtains.

We were sure my mother had reached from the great beyond and taken him with her to the hereafter. I knew my parents were both together now, and at peace.

Since then, I've received other signs. One stands out. I was walking the beach and having a mental conversation with my dad about a serious problem. When I asked for a sign, just as the sun was setting a rainbow broke through the clouds, even though we'd had no rain. ♥

When I was tiny, maybe three or four, I asked my favorite aunt where I was before I was born. Her answer: "In God's pocket." Then I wanted to know where I'd be after I wasn't here any more, and she said, "Angels will come and carry you back to God's pocket." To this day, that simple explanation brings comfort. At the death of her toddler, Jessica, Cindy Macedo-Eggen of Bishop, California, had no trouble believing a child's report that angels took Jessica away. As Cindy says, "I choose to believe."

JESSICA'S ESCORTS

A man stopped my husband, Eric, one night when he was out on a job. The man gave his condolences for the loss of our daughter, Jessica, who had been killed in an accident at her daycare center. Coincidentally, the man said he knew the mother of a four-year-old who was also at the center the day the ice-burdened roof collapsed.

When this woman picked up her daughter that day, the little girl said, "Jessica's fine. Right after it happened, the sky opened up and three angels came down and took her up to heaven. She's fine."

The man told my husband that the young girl was very explicit. She described in detail what the angels were wearing and even what they wore on their feet. My husband, dumbfounded, thanked the man, and said goodbye.

A couple of nights later, some friends came to visit. They told us a story they had heard from a man who was on the scene immediately after the incident. He said that while he was trying to pull the large chunks of ice off Jessica, a little girl came up to him and said, "Jessica's not underneath there. I saw the angels come and get her. She's not underneath there."

Other stories have come to me, too. Letters have been written about the beautiful sunlight that came through the church windows during the service for our precious little angel. I had been so worried that my baby's spirit was still at the daycare center, waiting for me to pick her up. My first reaction was to try to find these people and get every detail, hear every word.

But then I decided, no, it doesn't really matter. What is important is what I choose to believe. And I choose to believe that my baby Jessica was escorted to heaven by three angels. ♥

Nurses who specialize in providing hospice care, I believe, are angels. Their love shines through every pain-reducing injection, every thoughtful word, every caring touch. In fact, they establish unique relationships with those they serve that do not end when life does. One such angel, Diana Peirce of Barre, Vermont, shares two special stories from her many memories.

DIANA'S STORY 1:

DECK THE TREES WITH LIGHT AND LOVE

After about four months in hospice care, David, age 28, died of AIDS. In rural Vermont, in 1988, both prejudice and fear about HIV were widespread. David's homecoming had been difficult but was made easier by the welcoming arms of parents and siblings. He suffered greatly during his illness, making his death seem, to those who loved him, almost a relief.

David and I shared a love of music and nature and of

Christmas. The poignancy of his death was made even more acute, as it occurred about two weeks before that special Holiday we both loved.

Christmas Eve dawned gray and cloudy. As I drove to my first patient of the day, I noticed that the freezing mist had left a shimmering coating on the bare trees that covered the mountains visible from the road. Thoughts of David filled my mind, and I think I may even have said aloud, "Oh, David, how you would have loved the sight of these trees!"

Just at that moment, a tiny hole opened in the overcast sky, and a single sunbeam glided down the mountainside. It created a glittering light, more beautiful than any holiday lights I've ever seen.

David, who died before the celebration of Christmas, was sharing in the holiday, just the same.

DIANA'S STORY 2:

SING TO ME A TUNE OF FAREWELL

Meg, a wonderful woman, died from breast cancer at the age of 42. Active in many areas of her community, Meg was beloved by all who knew her. A friend had created a ceramic mobile. Each hanging element of it symbolized one of Meg's contributions: mother, pianist, emergency medical technician, etc. As Meg's hospice nurse, I visited frequently and spent many hours with Meg in the room where the mobile hung. No matter where the mobile was suspended, I would manage to brush against it, causing a sweet tinkling sound. My ability to set the mobile moving was a joke between us, and its gentle sound became a treasured part of every visit.

A CHERISHED FRIEND

Meg became my friend as well as my patient.

Her death came early one morning, attended by her husband and children. I was also privileged to share the moment.

The next morning, a Sunday, I awakened earlier than usual and was drawn to venture downstairs, to the kitchen. In my kitchen window hangs a ceramic mobile, a gift from a friend. Its elements depict seashells, as the friend who fashioned it knows the ocean has long been a source of solace for me.

As I entered the kitchen that early September morning, I was all alone. My husband and children remained asleep. No windows were open, no air stirred. Yet, I was greeted by the sweet familiar sound of the mobile in motion.

I remain convinced, more than 15 years later, that the tinkling of my mobile was the gentle sound of Meg's final goodbye. ♥

When the general calls, the soldier reports for duty. Through the ages, parents have seen their sons — and, lately, daughters — go off to war. It is never easy, but sometimes when the cause is worthy, the parents take heart in knowing it's the right thing to do. Christian parents — who believe in their hearts that the Supreme General needs their child — can find the peace that helps heal their grief. Bereaved father Dwight Flegel of Fayetteville, Georgia, shares his story of loss and acceptance.

CHRISTIAN SOLDIER

Seven years ago, a bus hit and killed my ten-year-old son Justin. He was a twin and a real special kid. We are all Christians in my family, but Justin was very serious about being saved and witnessing to other kids. Sometimes the kids at school would make fun of him for this.

The day of the accident, a good friend was babysitting and left the boys playing as she completed her bus-driving route. As she passed her house on the way to the bus depot, she honked at the boys to let them know she was coming home. The depot, where many buses were converging, was only a block away. For some reason I'll never understand, the boys decided to run and meet her there.

I got the call and arrived at the scene just after the ambulance and fire truck. To watch his mangled little body being extricated from under the bus, and to know I could do nothing — these were the most helpless feelings in the world.

I went through all the stages of grief. One particular day, I was stuck in "anger." I sat in church, furious with God for having taken my wonderful son. Suddenly, I heard a loud "voice" in my head with two clear messages: "He's not yours, he's mine!" and "*I* needed him!"

I sat dumbfounded. Then, as our assistant pastor began to speak to the congregation, I saw a vision of what looked to be Jesus, standing next to a very large man dressed as a soldier. I didn't recognize the man until he spoke. It was Justin. He said, "Everything's cool, Dad."

I received a rush of understanding that put my heart to rest. My anger disappeared and I felt a peace about me. Later that same day, Justin's twin, Dustin, who knew his brother like himself, came up to me and said, "Justin is really happy, Dad." ♥

It doesn't matter at what age your parents die, it's still an enormous loss. Whether they're in their 60s or 90s, we miss them and are sad to see that chapter of life end. Robin Sigler of Virginia writes that her parents were 81 and 84 when they died — after lives lived well and long. Still, she welcomed the comfort that came from animals, especially birds, which her parents had loved.

A CHINESE PHEASANT

My parents had always been animal lovers, and in their senior years they became very involved with local "varmints." They had seven acres of property on the Chesapeake Bay on Virginia's lower peninsula, and they loved to feed day-old sliced bread to the wild raccoons from nearby wetland areas.

Mom and Dad also did lots of bird-watching and took on the project of raising a brood of baby Mallard ducks whose mother had been run down in the street. My parents kept these little feathered orphans in a large box in their kitchen, feeding them carefully until the weather warmed and they grew big enough to be in a large pen in the yard. For years after the adoptees had all grown and departed the property, single pairs of ducks would appear from time to time and waddle around in the yard. One of them would know just where the water bowl with grain could be found, and the mate would stand back suspiciously for a while, not knowing that this had been home to his duck friend.

When we visited my parents, they would tell us about the exotic markings on this or that species of bird that had been on the property lately, and how unusual it was for it to be seen in their area. My father was very proud of this piece of land that he had somehow been able to buy toward the end of the Depression years. It was the only home we four children had ever known and a delightful place to grow up.

THE WISDOM OF AN OWL

My father died when he was 81 years old. On the chilly autumn day of his funeral, I briefly left the crowd at their home and walked out toward his greenhouse, now very much overgrown. Apparently, my intrusion into this wooded setting disturbed a big owl sleeping on a branch high over my head. In a flurry of wings this huge bird flew off toward the waterfront and a quieter spot. I can remember thinking at the time that this owl represented my father's spirit.

A little more than three years later, my mother died in January, just after her 84th birthday. I can remember having asked her if she ever went to the cemetery to visit my father's grave. She said that he was not there, that he was on the property they loved so much.

COLORFUL COMFORT

A sister and brother of mine have homes that share my parents' waterfront area. Within a day or two of my mother's funeral, I was hearing reports from my two siblings about a brightly colored bird they had spotted in the wooded area near my parents' house. This rare creature turned out to be a beautiful, golden Chinese pheasant with flashes of yellow, red, and green in its plumage. It stayed on the property for about a year, intriguing all of us, and bringing us comfort. ❦

The "buddy bond" between father and daughter is a blessing for which I will be eternally grateful. And when our buddy dies, we daughters can find ourselves bereft beyond words. But if we choose to be open to signs of our father's unceasing love, we might find the comfort we need — sometimes when we least expect it. Here's what happened to Stacie Zinn of Naples, Florida, after her beloved dad died.

MY TRAVELING BUDDY

My father passed away after a failed heart transplant several years ago. He and I were extremely close, and his death was very difficult for me. I was with him at the time, a great blessing, I assure you.

Since his death, he has made it quite apparent that he is still with me. On the day I picked up his ashes from the funeral home, I was driving to my home with the box of his ashes on the seat next to me. I tried to get a song on the radio. Oddly, the radio refused to tune in anything, until I came across an old Jim Croce song, one of Dad's favorites. So I just said aloud, "Okay, if that's what you want to hear, we'll listen to it."

Later, on another day, I was driving again and felt his presence next to me. I couldn't see him but I knew for certain he was there. I began to cry, then he touched me on the shoulder and was gone.

On another occasion, my boyfriend, Rich, and I went to pick up my father's car from a friend of his who had it in his driveway for safekeeping. I was in my car and Rich was driving my father's car. Just as we were about to pull out of the driveway, I looked in the rear view mirror. It wasn't Rich in the driver's seat. It was my dad, smiling up and laughing with his friend.

Then, on the night of the premiere of a film for which I served as screenwriter, Rich, some friends, and I were driving to the screening. This was to be the first time anyone had seen my film on the big screen, a very significant event in my life. As we were driving up the highway, I looked over at a semi-truck coming up in the right lane. The driver smiled at me.

It was my father. ♥

Ever wonder why a "Deer Crossing" sign shows up at a particular place? A friend of mine says it's because deer can read and they want to cross where they're supposed to. I always smile when I imagine a deer as it romps along, stops to read the sign, then looks both ways before crossing the road. Susan Finnegan of Saugus, Massachusetts, writes about signs from her dear grandmother, Mamie.

DEER SIGNS
CAN BE DEAR SIGNS

I was taking a walk in Maine, asking for God's guidance. Three quarters of the way into my walk, I looked to the right, into a clearing, and saw a beautiful deer. Our eyes met and our gazes held for about three minutes. I experienced great peacefulness and serenity and felt that everything was going to be all right.

My beloved grandmother, Mamie, died April 1, 2000, from stage IV breast cancer. She was 88 years old and truly beautiful. I had asked my mom to call me right away when Mamie died, because I wanted to pray. Mom called me 10 minutes after Mamie passed away. I asked God to show me a sign: I wanted to see a deer before the day was out, to know that Mamie was at peace. But I thought for sure my request would be denied.

That night, I decided to go up to my mother's house to be with her and my sister. Driving up at dusk, I thought maybe, just maybe, I would see a deer. I saw nothing. I decided to forget the idea. Just then, I came upon a "Deer Crossing" sign. I laughed out loud. I had never noticed that sign before, but I knew that God chooses his own "signs," and that Mamie was at peace.

A few weeks later, while I was folding laundry, I pulled out a sweatshirt of my husband's that I hadn't seen for months. It had a beautiful deer applique on the front, and once again, I said to myself, "Mamie is at peace."

A Dream to Remember

Mamie came to me in a dream this week. She had on a beautiful white sweater and a blue ring. I was the only one who could see her. She said, "Oh, hi!" to me in an upbeat tone. Then she walked over to my grandfather and lovingly patted him on his head. My alarm went off at that point, and I now have the gift of remembering the wonderful dream. ♥

Something as simple as a perfect bloom in winter can lighten one's grief, writes Dr. Katharine Shields of Newman, Georgia, who felt sad one chilly morning soon after her mother died.

WINTER ROSE

When my mother died, a friend brought me a rose plant, instead of the usual funeral flower arrangement. I put it on the porch and forgot about it.

Several months later, I was missing my mother a lot, wishing I could hear from her. It was winter. There was frost that morning, with a very light dusting of snow. I poured myself a cup of coffee and sat down to look out the window.

There on the patio was my scraggly, leaf-bare rosebush. It sported one bright and perfect bloom — a beautiful, red rose. I felt secure that this was my sign. And my grief has been much lighter. ❦

We love our pets, and they love us. Dogs, especially, provide the kind of comfort that has earned them the title "man's best friend." A dog plays a prominent — and soothing — role in each of these two short pieces by The Rev. Dr. Gordon Douglas Postill, bereavement director for Hospice of Naples in Florida. His letter to me began, "I can see that death has touched and transformed you personally. I can certainly relate."

GORDON'S STORY 1:

WITH A BOUNCE IN MY STEP

Part of my summer vacation in recent years included returning to Kingston, Ontario, where just over a year earlier, my sister and I had scattered our mother's ashes over Lake Ontario.

As I walked over to the lake and dipped my hands in the water, everything went very much as I might have anticipated. I felt some sadness and loss, but mostly I felt embraced by feelings of gratitude and peace. But just when I thought I was ready to move on, I really began to miss my mom and found I couldn't leave.

Suddenly out of the corner of my eye, I noticed a Shetland sheepdog — a "sheltie" — playing nearby with its owner. A lovely scene in its own right, it had a profound meaning for me at that particular moment. Before she developed Alzheimer's disease, my mom had played regularly with her own sheltie, Corbett, in that very same location.

Some people might have dismissed this as just sentimental coincidence, but I knew far more was happening here. I also knew it was time to leave...with a bounce in my step.

GORDON'S STORY 2:

A Boy and his Dog

In World War II, Douglas was killed in action while serving as a U.S. Marine. Douglas' death was devastating to his parents, Edna and Jack, as he was their only child. His mother, in particular, became more and more depressed in her grieving until one night she had a dream.

In her dream, Edna saw Douglas as a young boy walking along a familiar path by the Grand River in Paris, Ontario, with his beloved dog, Blackie. The sun was just coming up, and the overall scene was quite beautiful and peaceful. Awaking from her dream, Edna knew instinctively that Douglas was all right and that she could begin to get on with her life.

Edna's experience is especially meaningful for me as she is my aunt and Douglas was my cousin. I am very proud to be intimately connected with him through my middle name. ❦

*We humans sometimes seem to have at least two sides: the
one we show to the outer world — the public side — and
the one we keep only for those who are closest to us —
the private side. Sometimes, it takes a lifetime to reconcile
the two. Martha Wakely of St. Joseph, Missouri, never gave
up. Eventually, she came to embrace all sides of her many-
faceted father.*

THE RED-WINGED
BLACKBIRD

My father died suddenly on March 17, 1998, in St. Joseph, Missouri. It wasn't just coincidence that he died on St.
Patrick's Day. I like to think that God's sense of humor coop-
erated, with Dad wearin' the green that St. Paddy's Day and
able to continue his charade, even through death.

Dad was born in Guadalajara, Mexico, in 1910, and for
many reasons I never understood, he denied that he was
Mexican throughout his life. His 6'2" stature, Roman nose,
fair complexion, and non-Hispanic surname — which he se-
lected upon becoming a U.S. citizen — helped him preserve

the façade.

Dad was a scrapper, a heavy drinker — a big, unapproachable, tough guy, very serious and never smiling. My earliest memories of our relationship revolve around efforts to appease the angry man who came home from work in a drunken stupor every Friday night. Sundays we spent taking long rides, as Dad tried to reconcile with Mom and my brother and me for his outrageous behavior. Both my brother and I were sensitive children, who — like all children — needed their Daddy. But he wasn't there for us.

Years passed, and we grew up without him. Thankfully, we had a loving family who pulled together to try to fill the void for us. I hated him and I loved him; I wanted so badly to be loved and cared for. I spent my teen years acting out rebelliously, as I tried to get even with Dad and repay the hurt.

GOD'S PLANS FOR HEALING

Many, many years later, when I was 53 years old, my father and I were able to talk about those hurtful years. This, after a lifetime of the denial and silence endured by families of alcoholics. God had a plan for our healing that was far beyond anything we had imagined. Mother developed

Alzheimer's disease. As a result, my husband and I brought my parents from California to Missouri to live nearby so that I could supervise their care. They were now both in their 80s.

On the morning after Dad's death, I spied a bird outside my kitchen window. The thought that entered my mind was, "That's just like my Daddy — the sleek red-winged blackbird, with its dark side and its brilliant side." That bird was comforting to me, as I sensed my father was letting me know that he was with God in his brilliance. I felt that all would be okay.

A red-winged blackbird has been there for me, too, in a tree outside the nursing home where Mother lives. It gives me reassurance that Dad's spirit is there watching over her, even after death. Other days when I have worries about my own life, there it is — sitting on a fence post as I drive along the country road where I live. I don't see it often, just when I need reassurance. That sleek beauty brings me comfort, as I am finally certain of my father's love and caring. ♥

It is no accident that "light" is associated with "love." We talk about the lovelights that shine in people's eyes, the beloved one being "the light of my life," or when the loved one walks into a room, the whole place "lights up." Diane Robson of Cambridge, Ontario, shares what she calls "a personal and spiritual vision that was, and still is, of great comfort to me following the recent death of my father."

DADDY'S LIGHT

I was very close to my dad. From the moment I was born, I was "the apple of his eye." The weeks after his passing were difficult for me. I missed him tremendously, and wasn't sleeping well. I continued to feel his presence in our bedroom, especially in the middle of the night.

On one of these occasions, I awoke and noticed a strange square of light on the wall. It was opening and closing at regular intervals. It was directly to the right of a picture of Jesus that had hung on our wall for years.

In the morning, I tried to make sense of it, but there was no possible way to logically explain the light source.

I experienced this peaceful glow on the wall for several nights, always at around the same time. The third night it appeared, I sat on the edge of the bed while staring at it. I decided to approach the wall, and as I placed the palm of my hand gently on the light, I whispered, " Daddy," and it was gone.

It has not appeared since. I truly believe that our spirits touched that night, and that my father was saying his own special "goodbye." Every time I look at that treasured picture on our wall, I smile, certain that my dad is free of pain and is, indeed, in a better place.

Just coincidence, or something much more? ♥

> *Friends can turn out to be closer than relatives. When you*
> *share your dearest hopes and your worst fears with*
> *companions, bonds develop that endure forever. According*
> *to Ella Brubacher of St. Jacobs, Ontario, all of Nancy's friends*
> *have talked about the comforting coincidences they*
> *experienced after Nancy died. Here's Ella's story.*

NANCY'S ANGELS

A few years ago, I lost a friend, Nancy Snyder, to cancer. Nancy lived alone, having been left by her husband several years before, so she relied on her girlfriends for companionship during her illness. In that time we spent with her, Nancy became a true inspiration in all our lives.

When her family was planning her funeral, her dad suggested to the minister that the pall bearers should be eight of Nancy's closest girlfriends, since they were the ones who "stuck by her" through her two-year ordeal: first with breast cancer, then reconstructive surgery, then ovarian cancer.

One of our friends had been exceptionally generous of her time with Nancy, especially at the end. I decided to run into the Angel Treasures store in our small town to pick up a special gift to let this friend know that I, too, cherished her friendship. I started telling the clerk about Nancy's death and broke into tears. Naturally, I was eager to get out of the store. The clerk handed me my purchase, then reached into a drawer and grabbed a handful of small pieces of jewelry. "Here," she said, "pass them around."

Bleary-eyed, I left the store. When I got to the car, I pulled what the clerk had given me from my pocket. They were angel pins — and there were exactly eight of them. Needless to say, we all wore angels on our lapels as we carried Nancy's casket to the grave for her burial. ♥

It's like a tape-recording — that "mother's voice" we hear in our minds. "Don't bite your nails. Mind your manners." These are lessons drummed into us from the earliest days of our lives. Sometimes, however, Mother's voice takes on special meaning. Elaine Graves of Rochester, New Hampshire, tells of an extraordinary experience just 17 days after her mother's death. "I have never had an experience like this before in my life," she comments.

THAT FAMILIAR VOICE

My mother died on April 1st. On April 18th, I was admitted to the hospital through the emergency room. During my stay, which was only three days, I kept talking to my mother. I said things like, "If you can hear me, Mom, please keep an eye on everyone and make sure that they are doing everything right, because I don't think I'm ready to pass over yet."

After the tests and procedures were over and I was just resting, I heard my mother's voice. She said, "Hi, it's Mom."

Just as she did when she called me on the phone. I could see her face as plain as day — the only time I have been able to see her face in my thoughts. Then she said, "Well, you sure have gotten yourself into a fine mess." This was a typical remark from Mom — blunt and to the point.

To this I answered, "Hi, Mom, how're you doing?" She said, "Fine." Another pat phrase of hers. I asked her how she liked it up there. "Oh, it's okay." That was her stock answer to every big question anyone ever asked her. We said things like, "Love you, miss you," and I said, "Please come back and visit me again," and she just faded away.

I'm sure that she was truly there with me. It wasn't just a dream. It was a beautiful experience, one I will always treasure.

I got to talk to my mom one more time. ♥

True Stories of Comforting Coincidences from Those Who Grieve | 3 |

When we see a rainbow, we are reminded of the legendary possibilities it implies: the pot of gold awaiting us at the end of the arc. When mourning a mother's passing, a daughter may find great treasure in the rainbow itself. Diane Paglia of Tewksbury, Massachusetts, tells how a double rainbow lifted her spirits.

AN IRISH BLESSING

My mother passed away on November 5, 1999. A few months later, I was starting down the street on my daily walk, when I heard someone say, "Diane" – just the once, and from what "felt" like behind me. I looked around at the neighbors' houses and behind the building on my left, then started back up the curve to my house. There was no one in sight.

It had been a woman's voice, in a normal tone – not loud or urgent. But I had heard it clearly, so I called out, but no one answered. Deeply puzzled, I continued my walk. Just as I was returning home, it began to rain heavily.

When the rain ended, the sun came out brightly and it was very warm. As I stood looking out my back door, I saw a beautiful rainbow — a double rainbow! It seemed to start far behind my house and go right over to my mother's house (she had lived in the same neighborhood).

My siblings and I had recently decided to sell my mother's house. We had struggled to make the right choice. I was thinking that St. Patrick's Day was approaching and how much my mother, being Irish, had just loved that holiday.

A POT OF GOLD

I was sure this was a message from our mother that her home was a "pot of gold" for us at the end of the rainbow. It also became clear to me that it was my mother calling to me earlier. It lifted my spirits. I felt she was telling me that our decision was fine, and that she wanted us to share in the benefits of her "pot of gold" — the home for which she and my father had both worked so hard. ♥

Why do lyrics from popular songs stay with us? Take "Someone to Watch Over Me," for example. Isn't it because the song speaks to a need that lives deep within us? Even the strongest, most independent individuals have moments of wishing there were someone to watch over them. Maybe to give a gentle nudge in the right direction when uncertainty takes hold, or perhaps just to "be there." Two stories by Jenette Bennett of Fayetteville, Georgia, remind us of that deep-seated need.

JENETTE'S STORY 1:

DADDY'S MESSAGES

My daddy died 26 years ago. He always called me "Suzie." It was his special nickname for me, and no one else has ever called me that.

Some years ago, he appeared to me in a dream. Standing in a doorway, he put his arm around me. He hugged me and said, "I'm sorry, Suzie." When I asked him why he was sorry, he told me my grandmother had died. It was not my grandmother, but my father-in-law who died, two days after that.

A few years later, he appeared in another dream in the same doorway. The message again was, "I'm sorry." I woke up before I could hear the name of the person who had died. This time my special uncle, Lyman, Daddy's brother, died unexpectedly the next morning. He had developed a blood clot following a minor surgery.

These were sad messages, but they were made easier by the knowledge that my daddy is watching out for me and knows my sorrows and cares for me still.

JENETTE'S STORY 2:
CAROL'S LIGHT

My cousin Carol and I, close in age, were raised together. She died a few years ago, leaving a grieving husband. After some time had passed, my husband and I arranged to go on a double date with a good friend of ours and Carol's widower, Jim.

I had been worrying about how Carol would feel about our helping Jim to meet another woman. I silently wished that I could have a sign that Jim's going out with someone else was all right with her.

In the guest room, I had a battery-operated lamp that looked like a candle. This particular lamp has to be twisted to make the bulb light. I went into the room to prepare for company and saw it was turned on. I unscrewed the bulb, and set the lamp back on the dresser.

Later, I told the friend who came to stay with us about finding the lamp mysteriously lit. When she got up the next morning, the lamp was burning again! She told me, "Last night, when I got into bed, I said to Carol, 'If that was you, do it again to let us know for sure.'"

Twice was enough to convince me that the double date was okay and that Carol watched over us. ♥

When heavy with mourning, our hearts may yearn for profound, dramatic signs of continued love from our dear ones. We don't always get what we yearn for. At least, not in the way we expect. Some messages are neither profound nor dramatic but simple and sweet, as this vignette from Ellen Courtemanche of Marco Island, Florida, shows us.

MARGARET'S M&M'S

My beloved mother, Margaret, had a sweet tooth beyond imagination. Her favorite treat was M&M's® candy.

At the age of 97, Mom died peacefully in a nursing home in Minnesota. I had moved her there from her home in Wisconsin, so she could be near my family and me.

A week after Mom's death, we traveled to Wisconsin for her memorial Mass. After checking into a lovely, clean hotel, I opened the drapes in our room. Something on the carpet caught my eye.

As I picked it up, I realized it was a piece of M&M's candy. Mom seemed to be right there in that room with us. ♥

We humans seem to thrive on symbols. Flags become more than pieces of cloth with interesting designs; they stand for courage, pride, belonging, and much more. Hearts symbolize love. Tulips symbolize spring. What symbolic meaning does the dove carry? Here's a story of serenity from Sonya Abramson of West Yarmouth, Massachusetts.

THE DOVE

Al was married for 45 years to my childhood and lifelong girlfriend. He had acted at times as a sort of "surrogate father" to my three daughters, and the children called the two of them "uncle" and "aunt."

Al developed prostate cancer and was given 10 years to live. He passed away a little bit short of that time. His death occurred while my husband and I were in Key Largo, Florida. Because of my terror of flying, I was unable to return to Massachusetts in time to attend the wake and funeral. Emotionally, I fell apart.

On the day of Al's burial, I sat out on my deck, sobbing uncontrollably. A dove flew down from a nearby tree, landed at my feet, and stayed with me for about 10 minutes. I had a long, tearful conversation with it. I believe that it was Al, coming to tell me it was okay that I missed his funeral. I began to feel much better and found myself smiling through my tears.

A month later, we made our annual trek to another part of the state. We had settled in and were relaxing on the 10th-floor balcony, when a mourning dove appeared on the railing. This dove continued to come back during our stay. Of course, I don't know that it was the same dove, but it was there — and I chose to believe.

These dove visits occurred repeatedly over the years. The last time the dove appeared, it stayed for about five minutes while we cooed to one another. Needless to say, my husband thought I was nuts. The dove never returned. I felt at peace. I believed Al was telling me he was okay now.

Fifteen years ago, I went with my husband to visit his family in Israel. In Bethlehem, I purchased five mother-of-pearl dove pins. According to Christian tradition, the dove is the symbol of the Holy Spirit, and of understanding. Since Al had connected with me in that form, I gave the pins to his widow and family and to others who loved him. They treasured their pins, and have since adopted the dove as a symbol on greeting cards and other items. It brings them solace.

Last fall, my husband and I both had cervical spine surgery to correct problems stemming from different causes. My loving girlfriend, Al's widow, said, "Don't worry, the dove is watching over you."

This symbol has become part of our lives — all because a dove dropped gently down to a deck in Key Largo, on the day that Al's spirit was set free. ♥

Ever work really hard to solve a problem then, once you have the "aha" experience, you realize the answer lay right in front of you all the time? "Of course," you say, "why didn't I see that before?" That's how some of life's greatest lessons come to us. Some stories of comforting coincidences also contain profound messages in the simplest form. This one, from Jean Hewitt of Ft. Pierce, Florida, certainly does.

GEESE IN FLIGHT

After patiently and courageously enduring a lengthy illness, my mother slipped away peacefully three days before Thanksgiving. One late afternoon, the family was completing the funeral plans. We were just leaving the cemetery plot when suddenly a large flock of geese flew overhead, winging their way south.

To us, this was a comforting reminder that God is in heaven, all is right with the world. Life goes on.

Several months later, while walking alone near my home on a spring day, I again spotted geese. I imagined they were the same flock, now on their return journey. As I watched, they changed the V formation of their flight. Some birds from the rear moved forward, and the birds previously leading the flight moved back.

As I thought about this interesting sight, I began to see a parallel for humans. The roles that we play change as life goes on, and we assume responsibilities once borne by others. God watches over us all the time. All is well. ♥

Grandparents frequently develop their own way to remind us of their presence. While growing up, Glenda Turnage of Chester, California, was used to getting a gentle swat on the behind from her affectionate grandma. But imagine Glenda's surprise when a love pat comes "out of the blue."

GRANDMA'S LOVE PAT

On April 11, 1998, my grandmother died at the wonderful age of 94. I, at 38, felt so lucky to have enjoyed this lovely lady in my life for such a long time. I shared so much with her, all my dreams for the future, as well as my sorrows. Throughout my entire life I knew, no matter what I did, she would always be proud of me. She gave me the greatest gift: unconditional love.

While Grandma was alive, only one aspect of my life was unfulfilled: I did not get my career off the ground. She saw me through the challenges of graduating from college, but she didn't live long enough to see me put my knowledge to work. My heart ached that she would not know that I achieved success in my career as a hospice nurse.

Although I sat with Grandma when she took her final breath, I felt I had lost her long before that moment. She experienced bouts of delusion during the last months of her life, so that the Grandma I knew wasn't really there. It broke my heart to lose the support I had counted on for so long.

GLIMPSES OF GRANDMA

Soon after her death, I felt her in my presence daily. As I worked around the house, I could swear that I glimpsed her out of the corner of my eye. When I finally got the job I had worked for so long and so hard, I knew her support for me had helped me reach that moment.

One evening, I was chatting with my husband about my new position. I felt a tap on my behind and thought, at first, he had done it. But he stood too far away. My hairbrush slid from my hand. "Grandma is here," I said. "She just hit my butt!"

He stared at me. Then I ran into my daughter's room. I was crying and yelling all at the same time. Then I calmed myself a bit so I wouldn't scare her. "Grandma hit my butt," I told her.

"She always does that," my daughter said.

Then it hit me: my grandmother was still there for me.

I feel her often and am comforted by the knowledge that I can still count on her support. ♥

Lynn Smith of Waterloo, Ontario, and her mom were as close-knit as a mother and daughter could possibly be. Understandably, Lynn felt a huge void in her life — and in her heart — after her mother died. But Lynn found sweet solace and a renewed resolve after several unusual but reassuring occurrences.

SWEET SOLACE
FROM MOM

Mom struggled with diabetes and heart disease for a very long time. Slowly, painfully, she gave up the fight. It was the saddest day of my life when I held her hand for the last time. She held my hand in the moment of my birth, and I held hers in death.

Several strange yet peaceful things have happened to me since her death, and I wasn't sure at first whether to attribute them to coincidence or to Mom.

A Sign from a Lowly Ant

The first such incidence occurred at her graveside. I was in a particularly depressed state and went to her grave, sat down, and began a litany of boo hoos. Plus, I wanted to share a cigarette with Mom, one of our mutual enjoyments. As I sat on the grass looking down at her headstone, I felt desperate for confirmation that Mom was listening and could somehow help me with my difficult situation. As I cried, I begged her to give me a sign that she could hear me. I looked down at the gravestone, and one tiny little ant sat there all alone and made no move to crawl to the safety of the grass.

I believe the little ant was a sign from Mom. I left her graveside that day and have never returned. Since that day, I have known that Mom is all around me, not in the ground but with me.

A Visit
in the Garden

The next coincidence took place that spring. I've always loved spring, as it's a time when everything is fresh and new.

I find it invigorating to get out there with my spade and

flowers and convince myself that this year's gardening effort will be the best yet.

I was crouched down, digging little holes in preparation of planting, when out of the corner of my eye, I noticed something fluttering around me. I thought it was a bee, and my hand shot up in protection. Then I saw it was a beautiful butterfly. Not just a passing butterfly, but one that swooped and swirled around my head. I sat back on the grass while it circled me for at least ten minutes. As I talked softly to it, I began instinctively speaking to my mother.

The spirit in that butterfly was constant and serene. It stayed with me that day. I have not felt so comforted since Mom's passing. I have never before had more than a fleeting glimpse of a busy butterfly, but what happened on that spring morning was a visit from my mother.

Now, every spring I look for butterflies. This past summer while I was sitting on my patio, my visitor returned for a repeat performance, although this time its visit was shorter. I don't need such an elaborate demonstration anymore.

THERE WHEN I NEED HER

Sometimes, when I really need her, and sometimes when

I feel particularly alone, like at Thanksgiving and Christmas, I can hear Mom's voice saying, "Buck up, sweetie, you have your family and everyone is healthy. Nothing stays the same, but look at all the good times we had to remember. I love you, Lynn. You're doing a good job." ♥

Footnote: My heart goes out to Lynn. Since she shared this story, her daughter, Sarah, died suddenly and tragically. To add to her enormous grief, Lynn's best friend has since died of cancer.

Lynn, you shared your stories for this book with the intention of helping to comfort others. May the other stories appearing on these pages, bring <u>you</u> the added comfort you so dearly need.

Mary Walker of West Bloomfield, Michigan, is a hospice nurse who has witnessed many instances of comforting coincidences in the families she has served. Open to the significance of such signs of unceasing love, Mary was delighted at the way her own mother chose to communicate <u>her</u> undying love.

MOM LIGHTS MY WAY

Mother was a 25-year breast cancer survivor, so when it became clear that her illness was terminal, it was difficult for all of us to accept.

During her final month, I took time off from work to care for her at my home. Doing this brought me a sense of closure. Mom and I hadn't had the greatest relationship. Dad was an alcoholic, and while I was growing up we all kind of muddled through life the best we could.

I cared for Mom when she first battled cancer 25 years earlier, so I was grateful that I could be there for her during her valiant final fight.

One day my sister and I sat at Mom's bedside when she became quite agitated and began to describe some men she saw standing in the room. My sister and I said we didn't see anyone, and Mom got angry. "They're right there. The ones in the long white robes. Can't you see them?"

She told us the men were calling to her, beckoning her to join them. She said a partition seemed to be separating her from the men. "But they're right there," she insisted. "And they keep telling me to come here."

PLANS TO SEND A SIGN

Soon after that, I talked with Mom about sending a sign after she died. I asked her to find a way somehow to let us know she was okay, and she promised she would try.

A few days before she died, the light in the hallway leading to the family room — where Mom stayed — went out, and my husband and I made a mental note to fix it.

Early the morning Mom died, something woke me up, and I immediately went to her side. She was still alive, but her breathing was labored, and I knew death was imminent. I stayed by Mom's side all day. I took a quick break to go upstairs to get dressed. As I ran back downstairs toward Mom's room, she took her last breath. I felt a twinge of regret that my timing was so poor, as I had truly hoped to be with Mom at that sacred moment of death.

Early that evening I was sitting in the kitchen, when the light from the family room hallway flashed on and off. It seemed brighter than ever. My husband and I hadn't fixed the light, so we were puzzled about its sudden brightness.

The next evening, our hospice nurse called, and I recounted our experiences with the mysterious light. She and I laughed about how this might be Mom's sign to us. As if to confirm our suspicions, the light flashed on and off just before I hung up the phone.

I know that this was Mom's way of telling us that she was okay. It was her sign that she was fine. And the significance of her choice of communication brought me added comfort. What are the chances that a lamp would burn out as she was dying, then suddenly regain its power — and with such brilliance — after she died?

LOVE CONTINUES TO SHINE

Death to me is like birth. Both processes involve major suffering. But the end result is just as phenomenal. Mom's mysterious light reinforced this belief for me. I know that Mom's love continues to shine for us all.

This is particularly true for my little niece, who was only two when her grandmother died. My sister told me that shortly after Mom died, two-year-old Augusta woke up one morning and walked into their bathroom. My sister asked her why she was up so early, and Augusta replied, "Grandma woke me up." My sister looked at her quizzically, and Augusta added, "Grandma said, 'I love you, Augusta.'"

My sister and I agreed that this would be typical of Mom. She was a fabulous grandmother when all her grandkids were young, but by the time Augusta was born, Mom's cancer had reached an advanced stage, and she wasn't well enough to spend much time with Augusta

Death is not the end for any of us. I believe Mom is still in our lives — especially when we need her. ❤

*When Lydia Frescaz of Midland, Texas, heard that I was
compiling a book of people's comforting coincidences
following the death of someone dear, she was quite excited
and called to ask if she could share more than one experience.
Lydia explained she is a firm believer in staying open to the
significance of even the smallest synchronicity following
the death of someone dear. Such coincidences, she says,
help her find meaning and purpose in life. Here are her first
five stories. Lydia promises to share more in a future edition
of AFTERGLOW.*

LYDIA'S STORY 1:

MY FATHER'S FOOTSTEPS

When I was six years old, my dad was murdered.

I didn't understand death, and I thought he would come
home soon. Seeing Daddy in the casket at the funeral home
still didn't convince me he was gone forever.

Dad loved sitting in his rocking chair in the living room; he
was the only one who ever sat there. After he died, I heard
his chair rock at night. Then I would hear footsteps. I thought

he was blessing us, the way he used to after we were all in bed, but I was also afraid that I was hearing things. Mom was asleep, so I knew she wasn't the one making these sounds.

I was reluctant to tell anyone what I heard because I thought no one would believe me. They'd think I was just a silly little six-year-old missing her father. Then my quiet brother, Jessie, who hardly ever said anything, let it slip that he had also heard the rocking chair and footsteps.

So I knew in my heart that it was my father watching over us, protecting us and still blessing us. I know that, to this day, Dad still comes around when I need him – to visit and reassure me. ♥

LYDIA'S STORY 2:

COREY'S VISIT

My son, Corey, handsome and tall, had long, beautiful hair and a contagious laugh. He was so different that you could not help but notice him.

Corey was only 28 years old when he died unexpectedly from an asthma attack.

I was in shock. Corey was so full of love and spirit. He

used to write or call me often, to tell me his dreams and his plans for returning to his home state. As it turned out, only his body returned home — and that was for his burial.

I was devastated. His absence left a huge hole in my heart.

Soon after Corey's death in May 1997, my daughter Becky and I were eating a sandwich at the kitchen table. Suddenly Corey was there with us — we both saw and heard him. He said he had come to let us know he was okay, and that his love was right here with us. ❥

LYDIA'S STORY 3:

ANGELA'S ICY FAREWELL

My daughter, Angela, had so much to live for. Even though she was estranged from her abusive husband, she showered affection on her infant son, Bradley, and prepared for the birth of a new child in just three and a half months. All that changed in a split second of horror.

Angela lived for 10 days after her husband shot her three times. While in the hospital fighting to survive, Angela told me all she could think of was her son. She wanted to live and be his mommy. I tried, throughout this terrible ordeal, to focus on Angela's love, her smile, her laugh, her dreams for the future.

Later, I knew, I'd have to be the one to explain to little Bradley why his father was in prison and why he would never know the little sister his mother was carrying.

One morning as my husband and I slept, a chill gripped my body, as if ice-cold water was poured over me. I shivered so much that my husband woke and tried to warm me. Then the icy blast shifted to him and I did what I could to warm him. Soon the frigid feeling left him and returned to me. Then it was gone.

I knew that my Angela was using this way to communicate with us. She died at 6:30 that morning.

The bond I'd always had with Angela remained strong. During her life, when she phoned me, I would usually know before I answered that Angela was on the other end. Now, since her death, I know she visits us. I can smell the perfume she always wore. I feel her presence.

Bradley, as a baby, felt Angela's presence. Often he would laugh and laugh while he reached his little arms toward the ceiling. I knew that he was playing with his mommy. He was the love of her life, and she was still there to take care of him. He was such a well-behaved baby. I never worried about him, knowing that he had not only me to protect him but also his mother, as a special angel to watch over him. ❤

LYDIA'S STORY 4:

ERMA'S BIRTHDAY CARD

My cousin, Erma, and I were so bonded throughout our growing-up years that we acted like sisters. Even though we lived in different states as adults, we remained close in spirit. We wrote often and visited whenever possible, each time picking up as if we'd seen each other just a few days before.

The last time she came to visit me, I could tell something serious was going on in her body. She told me she was taking antibiotics for infection, but when I looked at her discolored skin, I knew it wasn't infection. When she returned home, her doctor confirmed that she had cancer.

I prayed that she could win the battle, for the sake of her two children, who still needed her. But after two years of thinking the cancer was in remission, she was told the cancer had spread and she was terminal.

I visited her in Oklahoma, taking my children with me. For nine days I did everything I could do to comfort my precious "sister." To answer the inevitable question of "why me?" I told her that God needed someone special like her to help with organizing things in Heaven. "God knows how efficient you are and he needs an angel like you to help him."

"You know just the right things to tell me," Erma said.

My nine days with Erma taught me to enjoy and treasure whatever time I had with my dear sister. When it was time for me to take my children back to Texas, I cried all the way home, knowing that I had seen her for the last time.

Erma died on July 6, and I grieved for my friend, my sister, my devoted cousin I loved so much.

A little over a month later, as I was loading the washing machine, a letter fell from the shelf above. I opened the envelope and saw a birthday card Erma had sent me years before. I then realized that today was August 11– my birthday.

I knew Erma had caused that envelope to fall to attract my attention. She wanted to wish me a happy birthday and reassure me that her love would always be with me. ❤

LYDIA'S STORY 5:

GRANDFATHER NEEDS A DRINK

My grandfather was a special person in my life. A proud worker, he knew firsthand all about hard times. I loved listening to the stories he told, stories about the past when things were so different. Even his jokes were special, because he had a great sense of humor.

In his later years, he got depressed. Work was his life and once he retired, the joy seemed to go out of him. But when someone would come to visit, he'd insist that they drink with him and be merry. "Bring me a drink," he'd shout playfully, in a tone that only Grandpa used.

He got sick and was diagnosed with prostate cancer. After hospitalizations and surgeries, he was forced to wear a bag under his clothes. This embarrassed him, but I reassured him that nobody would notice it. Still, he was uncomfortable, so he stayed home by himself more and more. On November 5, 1985, at the age of 90, he died.

Some time after that, one evening I was putting my children to bed while my husband watched TV in our den. Part of the ritual of getting my kids down for the night involved their last drinks of water. I stood at the water dispenser, filling their glasses, when I heard a voice from the den, "Give me some water." I finished taking care of the children, then went back to the dispenser for the drink to take to my husband in the den.

"What's this for?" my husband asked. "I didn't want any water."

"If you didn't ask for it, who did? I heard a voice coming from the den and you're the only one here." I smiled. Grandpa would have requested a drink in just that way. ♥

We all know people who seem never to find happiness in
their lives. How reassuring it would be to know that after
their earthly journey ends, perhaps they do indeed find the
joy that eluded them for so many years. Karen Masino of
Marco Island, Florida, tells of her experiences following
the death of her unhappy mother-in-law.

HAPPINESS...
AT LAST

My husband, Doug, and I had been married for 24 years
when his mother, Margaret, passed away. We didn't live in
the same state, but our distance from each other was more
than geographical. We were never really close; the only bond
we shared came through Doug and our children, her grandchildren. She was no closer to her other three daughters-in-
law. Just as in my relationship with her, all they had in common were the spouses and grandchildren.

Margaret's mother, from everything I'd learned, was not
a happy person. She was unable to show her daughter any

affection, never mind love, so Margaret's inability to warm up to people came as no surprise. Unhappy mothers raise unhappy daughters.

PREPARATION FOR UNDERSTANDING

About 20 years before Margaret's death, I awoke at 6:00 one morning in tears from a nightmare. In my dream, my younger sister had died and I was begging her to stay here on earth with me. She insisted that she had to leave. Although I kept pleading, she only smiled and said she had to leave.

I've always had an extremely close relationship with my two sisters, so close that this dream frightened me. At the time, one of my sisters, Dana, was a flight attendant. I knew that her flight from Honolulu to Dallas was due to arrive at 6:00 a.m. I managed to be patient for a couple of hours but finally called our older sister, Ann. "Has Dana come home yet?"

"No. Why? Is there a problem?"

I told Ann about the dream. "Please call me when Dana gets in."

At two o'clock, Ann phoned. The first words out of her mouth were: "Dana's okay, but she's in the hospital."

My heart leapt into my throat while I listened to Ann. "During the flight from Honolulu, she collapsed in pain. Her temperature was very high. She went immediately to the Dallas hospital. They diagnosed an ovarian cyst, which ruptured. She's on antibiotics, IV."

I relate this story now because it prepared me for another vivid dream, this time about Margaret.

RADIANT REFLECTIONS

After a long illness, Margaret died on a Monday. My husband flew immediately to Florida while I made flight arrangements so that I could arrive there about the same time as our out-of-state college children. For two nights, Doug slept alone in Margaret's bedroom. When I arrived, I slept in the other twin bed next to Doug's. Although I awoke the next morning in tears, I couldn't wait to tell Doug and the rest of the family the happy news of my dream.

In my dream, I was in Margaret's bedroom. I gazed into her dresser mirror and saw the reflection of someone sitting on one of the twin beds. I turned around and realized I was looking not only at Margaret but also at her mother.

Each of the women looked at me with beautiful smiles

---

and a sparkle in their eyes like I've never seen in my life. Margaret kept telling me how happy she was. Her mother never said a word but smiled the whole time.

I laughed and begged her to stay right where she was so I could get Doug to come in and see them. She promised she would. She continued to smile with what I would call "radiance." She just looked so happy and excited that I couldn't keep from laughing, myself. Then I awoke.

I feel that since she had been so unhappy in life, she wanted me to know that she was now, at last, happy. I can never forget her smile, those twinkling eyes, the obvious "radiance" in her appearance, and the repeated assurance of her happiness.

Because either Doug never dreams or doesn't recall them when he does, Margaret chose me to receive her message. I consider myself very lucky to have dreams and the ability to remember them.

In the seven years since her death, I've not had another dream like it. I pray every night that I'll always remember that dream. It was a beautiful message. ❤

As Marianne Bono of Tallahassee, Florida, shared the remarkable story of her two-year-old son's connection with her beloved father, she described the event as though it had happened yesterday. Her son is now 24 years old, yet the incredible experience is forever etched in her mind — and in her heart. In Marianne's second story, "Unbroken Chain of Love," she tells why she believes her parents' love and protection abide, even though they are no longer here in the flesh.

MARIANNE'S STORY 1:

GRANDPA'S GRAVE

When my father died in 1977, I was devastated. He was such a wonderful man and loving father.

I was eight months pregnant at the time, and I felt so bereft knowing Daddy would never see my child. My father died on June 27 and was buried on June 29, my birthday.

Amidst the enormous grief, I somehow found the strength to go on. A few weeks later, my precious son, Kris, came into the world, a sweet little bundle of joy.

There were many occasions when I wanted to take Kris

GRANDPA'S GRAVE

back north to Illinois to visit my Mom and family. I was also anxious to take Kris to my father's grave, so Daddy could finally "meet" his grandson. But I knew that traveling with an infant can be stressful, so I put off the trip until Kris was two years old.

AN INCREDIBLE OUTING

It was a beautiful, crisp autumn day when Kris, Mom, my sister, and I drove out to the cemetery. I hadn't been there since Daddy's burial two years prior, and I was struck by its vastness. It's one of the largest cemeteries in Illinois.

With Daddy's gravesite our destination, we were chatting away as we walked along the rolling grassy hills. Minutes later, to our dismay, it was clear that we were completely lost. My sister said she hadn't a clue which way to go, as she didn't often visit our father's grave.

But Mom was a frequent visitor, and she was becoming increasingly angry with herself for losing her way — and ours.

To add to our frustration, little Kris chose that exact moment to run off. I kept one eye on Kris as my sister and I helped Mom look at grave markers. Surely she'd find one that seemed familiar, which we hoped would act as a compass and point us in the direction we needed to go.

As Kris got farther away, I mumbled, "Rats, I gotta go after him." Mom was losing what little patience she had left as I ran toward Kris. I'll never forget the sight of my little guy, dressed in blue jeans, the green hood of his sweatshirt flopping up and down in the breeze as he sped forward.

GRANDSON AND GRANDFATHER CONNECT

Suddenly, Kris stopped. Something caught his eye, and he knelt down. As I came near, I saw his little forefinger moving across one of the flat gravesite markers, as though tracing shapes and letters.

I knelt down beside him. Kris was happily tracing his finger along the letters that formed my father's name. Two-year-old Kris had found his grandfather's gravesite!

I was so astonished that it literally took my breath away. Two-year-olds — and mine included — are too young to read. There was absolutely no viable explanation for his stopping at that particular grave marker.

That is, of course, unless Daddy and Kris were already so sweetly connected in a way that transcends our normal human understanding.

What surprised me most, I think, was my mother's reaction to this unexplainable event. Mom was a matter-of-fact, practical woman, who only seemed to see what was right in front of her. I never would have expected her to acknowledge the enormous significance of this incredible "coincidence."

But the look on her face told me she knew that what had happened was awesome beyond belief. Then she added matter-of-factly, "Well, he found his grandfather."

Indeed he had, and I whispered a loving prayer to my father: "Daddy, here's your little grandson." But in my heart I knew for sure that my Dad's spirit and Kris's had always been — and would always be — lovingly intertwined. ♥

MARIANNE'S STORY 2:

UNBROKEN CHAIN
OF LOVE

Mom died 15 years after my father. She suffered from a debilitating disease, and we knew her physical decline would be quick. But I was not prepared for her to die quite so soon.

The day she died, I had been to the nursing home to visit with her. But Mom was not one to share her feelings, say mushy goodbyes or have a fuss made.

She died right after I left her side, which filled me with regrets. Many "if only..." phrases churned inside me. The most painful one was, "If only I had stayed with her a few more minutes, I could have been with her when she took her last breath."

A JOYFUL DAY OF THE YEAR

Over the years as my feelings of regret and grief have diminished, I have reached a place of peace and serenity. In great part, this is due to the comforting coincidence of one date on the calendar: June 29. You see, Mom died on June 29, which is not only my birthday but also the date we buried Daddy.

I realize it is quite unusual to have such important dates within a family all converge on the same day on the calendar. And this synchronicity brings me great joy. It confirms for me that my parents continue to watch over me. It also reinforces that the chain of love that connects us is unbroken, even when our loved ones are no longer here in the flesh.

June 29 is not a sad day at all for me anymore. Instead, it's a day filled with endless love and gratitude. ❦

SHARE YOUR STORY

If you have experienced a comforting coincidence following the death of someone dear, please share your story with us for a future edition of *Afterglow: Signs of Continued Love.*

Mail your story to:	**Quality of Life Publishing Co.**
	P.O. Box 112050
	Naples, FL 34108-1929
Fax to:	1-239-513-0088
Email to:	afterglow@QoLpublishing.com

We'll accept a rough draft or even an outline. We're more interested in the "heart" of your story than in the manner of your writing/editing. Finetuning is OUR job! In fact, if you're better at telling your story than writing it, you can call us and tell your story to one of our editors. In the U.S., call toll free at **1-877-513-0099.** In Canada, call **1-239-513-9907.**

ABOUT THE AUTHOR

KARLA WHEELER is a lifelong journalist whose social mission is to help ease the way for those who grieve the loss of anyone special — a person or a pet. She specializes in writing about grief and other end-of-life topics.

Afterglow: Signs of Continued Love was inspired by the overwhelming grief she and her husband experienced following the back-to-back deaths of their fathers. Their dads died just four weeks apart — each of a different lingering illness. Although she was a woman of deep faith, Karla still found herself longing for a sign of continued love.

Readers of her newspaper columns, published across North America, were touched by Karla's examples of comforting coincidences and began sharing their own similar experiences. Hence, the book you now hold in your hands — a compilation of such stories, written from the heart, to help heal grieving hearts everywhere.

Karla has been a hospice volunteer since 1990, visiting with patients facing life-limiting illnesses and providing volunteer grief support to those who are bereaved.

Her first book on grief was published by Quality of Life Publishing Co. in 2001. It is an uplifting children's book entitled, *Timmy's Christmas Surprise.* Illustrated by Karla's young daughter, Jenny, the book tells the true story of a cat named Timmy and a family that

Photo courtesy of Penny Wigglesworth

Karla and her daughter, Jenny, pose with two Penny Bears. A portion of the proceeds of the sale of each AFTERGLOW book will be donated to The Penny Bear Company, a non-profit organization based in Marblehead, Massachusetts, which brings comfort and hope through hospices and children's grief camps.

felt sad after the death of their pet. The book, which includes bereavement tips for the holidays, provides a gentle springboard for discussions about loss through death. For information about this and other publications, log on to **www.QoLpublishing.com.**

Karla lives in Florida with her husband, Gerry, and their daughter, Jenny. Feel free to contact her via email:

afterglow@QoLpublishing.com

Grief is a process,

not an event.

Please be gentle with yourself

as you journey along that sacred path

known as grief.

HOSPICE CAN HELP

If you or someone you know is bereaved, please consider contacting your local hospice. Many hospice and palliative care organizations offer free grief support programs to members of the community.

TO FIND A HOSPICE NEAR YOU:

IN THE U.S.: Visit the web site of the National Hospice & Palliative Care Organization at **www.nhpco.org**. Or call the NHPCO at **703-837-1500**.

IN CANADA: visit **www.cpca.net,** the web site of the Canadian Palliative Care Association, or call **800-668-2785**.